CW00662160

Bonnie Dundee. A novel.

Max Beresford

Bonnie Dundee. A novel.
Beresford, Max
British Library, Historical Print Editions
British Library
1890
2 vol. ; 8°.
012631.g.13.

The BiblioLife Network

This project was made possible in part by the BiblioLife Network (BLN), a project aimed at addressing some of the huge challenges facing book preservationists around the world. The BLN includes libraries, library networks, archives, subject matter experts, online communities and library service providers. We believe every book ever published should be available as a high-quality print reproduction; printed on- demand anywhere in the world. This insures the ongoing accessibility of the content and helps generate sustainable revenue for the libraries and organizations that work to preserve these important materials.

The following book is in the "public domain" and represents an authentic reproduction of the text as printed by the original publisher. While we have attempted to accurately maintain the integrity of the original work, there are sometimes problems with the original book or micro-film from which the books were digitized. This can result in minor errors in reproduction. Possible imperfections include missing and blurred pages, poor pictures, markings and other reproduction issues beyond our control. Because this work is culturally important, we have made it available as part of our commitment to protecting, preserving, and promoting the world's literature.

GUIDE TO FOLD-OUTS, MAPS and OVERSIZED IMAGES

In an online database, page images do not need to conform to the size restrictions found in a printed book. When converting these images back into a printed bound book, the page sizes are standardized in ways that maintain the detail of the original. For large images, such as fold-out maps, the original page image is split into two or more pages.

Guidelines used to determine the split of oversize pages:

• Some images are split vertically; large images require vertical and horizontal splits.
• For horizontal splits, the content is split left to right.
• For vertical splits, the content is split from top to bottom.
• For both vertical and horizontal splits, the image is processed from top left to bottom right.

0 / 2 6 5

BONNIE DUNDEE.

VOL. I.

NEW AND POPULAR NOVELS

AT ALL THE LIBRARIES.

———

SLIDING SANDS. By HENRY CRESSWELL, author of 'A Modern Greek Heroine,' &c. 3 vols.

THE CRITON HUNT MYSTERY. By Mrs. ROBERT JOCELYN, author of 'The M. F. H.'s Daughter,' &c. 3 vols.

THE KEEPER OF THE KEYS. By F. W. ROBINSON, author of 'Grandmother's Money,' &c. 3 vols.

ALL FOR NAUGHT. By WILFRED WOOLLAM, M.A. 3 vols.

TWO ENGLISH GIRLS. By MABEL HART. 2 vols.

LONDON: HURST & BLACKETT, LIMITED.

BONNIE DUNDEE

A NOVEL

BY

MAX BERESFORD

There's lands beyond Pentland, and hills beyond Forth,
If there's lords in the South-land, there's chiefs in the North.
And wild dunnie-wassels three thousand times three,
Will cry hoigh! for the bonnet of Bonnie Dundee!'
                                        SIR WALTER SCOTT.

IN TWO VOLUMES.
VOL. I.

LONDON:
HURST AND BLACKETT, LIMITED,
13, GREAT MARLBOROUGH STREET.
1890.
All rights reserved.

TO MY SISTER MARY.

CONTENTS

OF

THE FIRST VOLUME.

BONNIE DUNDEE.

CHAPTER I.

ALISON DEAN.

A TRAP, followed by a large collie dog, drives rapidly along, rattling over the stones, and waking strange echoes in the High Street; and two ladies look up expectantly, prepared to bow to Dr. Murdoch as he passes them. But the doctor's face is turned in another direction; he is unconscious of May Lindsay's disappointed blue eyes, and the scornful set of her piquant little nose, as she exclaims:

'There goes Dr. Murdoch. I wish he wouldn't wear that hideous bonnet, though it does suit him. He looks just like Graham of Claverhouse in it. And he is like him in character; as brave and strong-willed. Bonnie Dundee! H'm! It would make him conceited, else I would call him so. What a flirt he is! Did you see, mother, he was so taken up looking at that mill-girl he had no eyes for us? He has given us the cut direct.'

'No doctor would do that, child, unless he had previously administered a polite anæsthetic,—least of all Dr. Murdoch; he is too canny for that. No, no, May, he didn't see us. Was that Alison Dean he was looking at?'

'Yes; she is pretty enough to attract him, I suppose, though she is only a mill-girl.'

Mrs. Lindsay turned her sharp little eyes on her daughter.

'And pray why shouldn't he be attracted by a good, bonnie lassie like Alison?

Don't let Dr. Murdoch hear you talk of her in that tone, May; jealousy may be flattering to a man, but it is ruinous to a woman. If you wear your heart on your sleeve, be sure the daws will peck at it till it's not worth having. As to Murdoch's liking Alison, you are quite safe—he'll do nothing so sensible. His wife will be the orthodox feminine inanity, with blue eyes and golden hair; a nose " tip-tilted like a flower petal " before marriage, and uncompromisingly pug after it. There! Don't speak; keep your temper and look pretty, and no man will ask more of you.'

Mrs. Lindsay's jerky little tirade ceased abruptly; and May tossed her pretty head, with its crowning wealth of gold, and walked on silently beside her mother, too insulted to reply.

The bell of the old church had just rung out, and the sound of its harsh clangour

was pealing and clashing overhead, start-
ling the sparrows from their perch under
the eaves, and causing the jackdaws and
rooks in the Abbey beyond to wheel and
skim about with answering tumult.

The mad rush and peal of the bell surged
overhead, and along the streets the busy
sound of feet hastening homewards was
heard. The mills had opened their doors
to pour into the streets the great mass of
workers, releasing them for one short hour
from the stifling air of the factory, the whirl
of machinery, the weary round of labour.

And there they were—bright-faced girls,
trim and happy for the most part, in little
knots of two and three turning busily home-
ward; sad-faced women with eager light
in their eyes, hurrying anxiously towards
the children whose voices the hum of shaft
and belt and pulley had not been able to
silence; hard-visaged men, whose faces were

too rugged for smiles; and eager-voiced
lads ready for life's struggles. All these the
bell summoned from the mills to fill the
muddy pavements of Arbroath with life
and stir and movement.

On a fine day the old town blossomed into
sudden beauty, and lay like a jewel with
many facets on the edge of the sea, shining
and glittering with a glory of clean streets
and bright houses. Then it was that the sea
led its ranks of white waves along the yellow sands, and the hills away at the mouth
of the Tay lay like a purple crown on the
water's brink. Then it was that the Common, and the fields in the distance, donned
a fresh green; and the boats, with their
brown sails touched to gold, came sailing
across the harbour bar into what was indeed
a fair haven. To the men in the boats, stern-
faced, keen-eyed, deep-voiced, no haven on
earth was fairer than this where the watch-

ful fishwives stood on the shore waiting their return, and where at noon the lads clustered on the harbour-walls to see the boats come in.

A fair haven it was on a summer's morning; but how fair when the storms rose, and the winds tore the waves into fury, none knew so well as the fishers who, away in the darkness, strained through the perilous seas for its quiet harbour. Then it was that every stone in the harbour came to be of value, that each homely shelter became more desirable than a king's palace, and the humblest roof was longed for, as men long for what is most precious in life.

But the bell has rung itself hoarse; it has ceased its clanging, and its echoes no longer vibrate through the streets that have become silent and deserted.

Mrs. Lindsay and May have disappeared; and Dr. Murdoch is driving on, thinking with interest of Alison Dean, and wondering where in the world he has seen her before. The doctor is himself an object of interest with his pale, clear-cut face, black curly beard, and keen grey eyes; but he is too familiar a figure to the inhabitants of the High Street to attract their observation, and Alison does not give him a thought as she passes along. The horse turns into a side street, and hurries its pace as if in sight of home; but the doctor's thoughts follow Alison's graceful figure and her young face under its tartan shawl. He never forgets a face once seen; and it appears to him that he has met those very brown eyes, red curling lips, and crimson cheeks before. But the picture is set in dainty lace and costly silk, and this girl is in the ordinary dress of the mills.

He knits his brows angrily;—it is so provoking to be haunted by a pretty face, whose beauty is not the property of any of one's own acquaintances; and how comes it that this girl is divested of the dainty surroundings that so naturally associate themselves with her?

Unconscious of the doctor's scrutiny, Alison passes on down the street and up towards the Abbey, under the old gateway of which she pauses to bid her companion good-bye.

The old arch, with its time-worn carving and red tones, made a quaint and pretty framing for the girl's bright face. A shaft of sunlight through the rain-laden clouds struck across it, bringing out the deep colouring of the sandstone; and through the open door there was a glimpse of columns and gravestones, an incongruous background to so fair a picture. But Alison stood in the foreground with the sunlight about her, and little knew that her life was to be shadowed by a mystery of sorrow

and death ; that the sunshine of love should
strike down to her by the grave of a mur-
dered victim ! She could not read the
future, and with a light heart she hurried
on to her attic in Well's Close. The little
room with its scanty furniture and air of
poverty seemed scarcely appropriate to a
girl of such refinement ; but it was evidently
no new home to her, for she hardly gave
it a glance as she entered. She crossed at
once to the window and threw it open,
leaning out an instant to gaze at a lilac-
tree and the distant cloud-flecked view of
the November sky. Then she stooped to
smell a rose in a glass on a window-sill—
the only pretty thing in the room beside
herself—and turned back smiling into the
homely interior, with a whispered name
that brought the colour to her cheek ; for
the rose was a present from Andrew Rayne,
the poet.

When Alison smiled, the whole place became transfigured, and one forgot the bare walls, their blank whiteness relieved only by a few rough sketches and a tiny book-case, in wondering at the occupant of the attic. There she stood—the ugly bodice and short skirt she wore utterly powerless to disguise the beautiful lines of her figure, altogether unable to dim the stedfast radiance of her young loveliness.

Beauty of face and figure she had in a high degree; but her chief attraction was not in this, but in the bright gentleness of her expression and the kindly flash of her brown eyes, which were altogether independent of exteriors. No gown, however hideous, could defraud her of her smile; no room, however bare, had power to quench the light of the frank eyes that looked so kindly on everyone and everything.

She turned now to preparing and eating her dinner; then she busied herself with little household cares, humming snatches of song all the time, with a voice that a blackbird might have envied; and when the room was as neat as hands could make it, and when she had finished her humble meal, she pinned her shawl over her head and made ready to go away to her work again.

At this moment a sound came up the stair, and a girl's voice called:

'Alison, Alison, are you no comin'? It's juist on the clap o' three.'

'Ay,' she answered, quietly. And, without further word, she crossed the room with light, even step, and, locking the door behind her, joined her companion at the foot of the stair. 'Jeanie,' she said, as they got out into the open air, 'what have you been cryin' for?'

'It's juist oor Liz,' said Jeanie, whose

red eyes had betrayed her. 'I think whiles she's like to brak' my heart. Puir lassie, gin she had a mither she wadna need sae muckle thocht.'

'What has she been doing now?' Alison asked, a grave look in her eyes.

'Nae mair than at ither times; but she's a fulish lassie, an' I'm whiles wae for her. Ye ken she winna listen to me, an' I doot ithers will lead her wrang. Gin she had a mither noo——'

'I think no mother could do more for her than you do,' Alison said, warmly. 'Liz is young enough still, and lassies are aye fulish-like; but she has a good heart, Liz, and you mustn't trouble over-much at her giddy ways; she is very young, remember.'

'Just that,' Jeanie sighed. 'But I canna help speerin' fat wad come to her gin I wis awa'.'

Alison did not answer. She was thinking how much less lonely she would have been if her own little sister had not died, but had lived to be, like Liz Munro, at once the comfort and the torment of her life.

Jeanie and Liz, like Alison, were friendless orphans, having lost their father at the same time; and it was this common bond that united Alison to them. Her father had been captain of the vessel in which Munro had sailed as one of the crew; the boat had gone down in a storm, and Captain Dean had perished with her. Munro died a few days later in the boat to which the crew had taken when their vessel foundered.

Mrs. Dean, a delicate, spiritless woman, did not survive the shock of her husband's loss: she died in a few weeks, leaving Alison, a girl of fifteen, alone in the world.

The orphan found a friend in Mrs. Munro, who took her home and gave her a daughter's place in her heart. For two years Alison's girlhood was sheltered with motherly care; and then the widow died, and the three girls were cast on their own resources.

Alison had then taken an attic for herself in the same land as Jeanie and pretty, wilful Liz; and there the three lived, working at the same mill during the day, and spending their evenings together for the most part.

Though none of them recognised the fact in words, there had always been a difference in thought and mode of life between Alison and her friends. Her innate refinement—for her mother had been a woman of culture—and superior birth could not but assert themselves; and though she associated with the other girls on the same footing, they instinctively accorded her the deference due to one in a higher position.

As for Alison, she was beginning to feel that her own life needed for its full development something larger than she could find in her present sphere; but she was not discontented.

Andrew Rayne lent her books, and at heart she was a philosopher, and could wait for the better life that some day should be hers. She had a sunny disposition that found a bright side to all dark experiences; and she laughed and sang through her troubles in a manner that was strange to Jeanie, who looked always on the sombre side of circumstances.

When they reached the large gates of the mill the two were at once surrounded by a group of girls, and it was easily seen that Alison was a favourite among them.

They gathered eagerly round her, and it was 'Oh, Alison, hae you minded the bit picture you promised me?' and 'Oh, Alison, oor Wullie's speerin' gin you'll gie him a sang the nicht.'

Alison's lips parted in a merry smile, and her eyes flashed as she heard half-a-dozen voices all speaking at once. Then she covered her ears with her hands and shook her head at them.

'You must remember I have only one tongue!' she said, her English accent contrasting with the broad Scotch of the other girls.

'No, Bell, your picture is not finished yet, but I have Tibbie's. There it is, Tibbie, and you mustn't mind that Jim is not in the *Saucy Tib* with the others. I couldn't put him in because he was away on the cliffs walking with you.'

Jim was Tibbie's sweetheart, and she

took the picture from Alison, blushing when the others laughed at the mischievous words. They crowded round to look at it, a rough little sketch in water-colour of a boat leaving the harbour. There was some truth of effect in the subject, and a curious grasp and realism in its treatment; but Tibbie did not look at it from the standpoint of the art critic. All she cared for was the white lettering, *The Saucy Tib, A. H.*, which proved beyond doubt that the boat was Jim's; and she gave a gratified smile as she gazed at it.

'You're awfu' kind, Alison. I'll hae to show it to Jim; it's real bonnie.'

Alison was already going into the mill, but she turned at a disappointed cry from Tibbie.

'Och, lassie! fat am I to say to oor Wullie?'

'Tell him I'll call in about seven,' Alison cried, as she disappeared within the dusty gates.

CHAPTER II.

HEART THROES.

As Alison passed into the mill, Dr. Murdoch's trap went by, and the doctor for the second time caught a glimpse of the pretty face that had aroused his bewildered curiosity an hour before. He had certainly met her somewhere. He could tell what she had worn: a quaintly-made gown of flowered silk, with ruffles of old lace at her throat and wrists, and a single rose in her black hair. He could not mistake the face, but he was puzzled to account for the difference in dress The girl he remembered was dressed and looked like a lady; this girl was a worker in the Ward Mill and wore the usual dress of her class. And yet he was certain they were identical. If he could only remember where he had seen that pretty girl in her quaint old costume! But he could not explain the enigma, and he turned to the groom beside him—

'Mearns, can you tell me who that tall, dark girl is?'

'Surely,' the man answered. 'It's juist Alison Dean; she's gey frien'ly wi' oor Wullie since he brak' his airm.'

'Whose lass is she?'

'Her feyther was a sea captain. He was drooned four years syne i' *The Marget.*'

'Is she Scotch?'

'Na, na. Her mither was athegither English—a puir, feckless body, that didna ken the worth o' a bawbee. She's awa noo far she disna want muckle sense or siller, God be thankit.'

'Good gracious! why should you thank God for that?'

'Weel, I'm thinkin' gin the Almighty only opened the door o' Heaven to the wummen fat hed siller or sense, there wadna mony o' them win in, puir, daft creatures. My ain Tibbie hasna siller, but she has eneuch sense to hae gotten a lad, an' I canna ask for mair frae a lassie.'

The doctor laughed.

'Has this Alison lived long in Arbroath?'

'Ou, ay—a matter o' ten years. She's a douce lassie, Alison, an' weel likit i' the mull. She's aye drawin' images for the weans an' singin' bits o' sangs for the lassies.'

'Does she sing, then?'

'Ay, does she. She has a voice almaist like oor precentor's—a gey, fine voice yon.

Gin ye're sleepin' some i' the sermon, yon
chappie waukens you as sune as he strikes
the Psalm.   We're no needin' ony organ i'
oor kirk, for he has an instrument i' his
ain throat !'

The doctor gave scanty attention to this
tribute to the precentor's voice.   He was
disappointed that Mearns did not help him
to solve the difficulty of his meeting with
Alison ; but he soon dismissed the subject,
and occupied himself with thoughts more
important than Alison and her history.

He went about among his patients that
afternoon concerned with nothing but the
cases under consideration, for he was just
passing through that epoch in a medical
man's career when the physician is first a
doctor then a man !   He was not yet
thirty, but his reputation had outstripped
his years ; his genius having claimed for

itself a recognition in professional circles as well as among the uncultured and indiscriminating.

In all Arbroath there was no doctor more popular than he; and he brought to bear upon his work an enthusiasm that insured his success in it.

As he went from house to house this afternoon, greeted with smiles and welcome from young and old, it seemed an impossibility that he should ever be anything but a favourite in the town. And yet, in a very few months, from these very houses would come a clamour for the life of the doctor, and the lips smiling now would be branding him as a murderer! But the shadow of the future was not yet thrown across the present, and Dr. Murdoch was still the people's friend and favourite.

May Lindsay, who was the daughter of

his partner, had at first turned up her
scornful nose at his success, and had said
that the secret of Murdoch's popularity
was in his cleverness rather than in his
skill. Personal liking for him had since
caused her to retract the words ; but, perhaps, skilful as the doctor undoubtedly
was, there was a little truth in the remark
that he owed his popularity to his cleverness, for there was something of genius in
the way in which he adapted himself to his
patient's idiosyncrasies. To them he ceased
to be 'the doctor,' and became 'oor doctor,'
a designation which, in spite of the thera-
peutic phase through which he was passing, witnessed more surely to the people's
trust in his human nature than any deference could have done. They cared for him
as a friend, and felt some sort of personal
responsibility for his success, even while
they stood in awe of his masterful exaction

of obedience, and his good-humoured cynicism and mockery of their fancied ailments.

As he stepped from the dog-cart before the gate of the Abbey House, his appearance suddenly underwent transformation. The alertness of his keen face gave way before a kindly interest. There was no cynicism in his glance now; for he had nothing but gentle consideration and cheerful encouragement for actual suffering, and he was just about to visit one of his favourite, because most afflicted, patients.

Mrs. Urquhart was not alone this afternoon, and the doctor raised his eyebrows in amused surprise at one of her companions—a tall, thin man with weak, colourless eyes; one of those men who for individuality are at the mercy of their clothes.

What the tailor could do for this one he

had done, for he was invested with all the attributes of velvet coat, baggy trousers, and an indescribable waistcoat. His hair fell to his shoulders, and he was extended in a limp diffuseness on an old oak chair; the unrelentingness of which was a mute satire on the character of its occupant.

Mrs. Urquhart's other visitor was May Lindsay, who sat at a little tea-table, her eyes all alight with mischief. They turned now to the doctor, and he gave them a swift answering glance of comprehension before he crossed to the sofa where his patient was lying.

'You see May is making tea for me this afternoon,' Mrs. Urquhart explained; 'and this is my nephew from London. You are just in time for a cup of tea, doctor; I daresay May will give you one.'

'Thank you,' he said, turning to shake

hands with May. 'I may as well confess
I came in on purpose for a cup; besides,
I guessed who would be dispensing tea to-
day.'

He gave the girl a meaning glance, and
May pouted to hide the happy blush of
which she was conscious. Mrs. Urquhart
watched the little by-play with secret
amusement—she suspected that the two
understood each other.

'I see that you have met before, then,'
she said. 'James, let me introduce you to
Dr. Murdoch.'

The man addressed half-rose, and held
out a languid hand to the doctor, who
secured the flabby member in a character-
istic grasp. Its owner looked mildly uncomfortable. With him, even discomfort
was a colourless sensation.

'Oh, ah, yass; if that is what is meant
by muscular Christianity, doctor, I would

rather not be a muscular Christian, don't you know ?'

'You are not likely to be muscular any-thing. Christian or pagan, it would be all the same so far as your muscles are concerned,' Dr. Murdoch said, bluntly.

'I daresay,' James drawled. 'In town we cultivate the higher life, you know.'

'Yes ? With any success?' gravely asked the doctor ; then, turning to May, 'I will trouble you for another lump of sugar, I think.'

'Certainly,' said May, promptly. 'Do let me give you two, Dr. Murdoch; I see you need a good many.'

'Thanks, one is quite enough. I am sweet by proxy—isn't that so ?'

The glance that emphasised the com-pliment was killing, and May blushed with pleasure.

'You are very absurd,' she replied, laughing.

'By proxy also?' he inquired, with a look towards the lank figure opposite.

May was afraid of betraying the merriment the question aroused.

'Have you seen the new poems?' she asked, taking up a volume from the table. 'Mrs. Urquhart is very proud of her nephew; it is a beautiful book.'

A faint glow suffused the face of the man before them.

'That is very good of you,' he murmured, and so betrayed himself as the author.

'Not at all!' May said, brusquely. 'Isn't it a beautiful book, Dr. Murdoch? Those white lilies on the gold ground are lovely.'

The doctor took the dainty volume she handed him, and read the title aloud.

' " Heart-Throes," by J. Dante Algernon.
Do you suffer from spasms, Mr. Algernon?
You should try Battley's Sedative Solution
—or laudanum, sixty drops to a dose—
either would be more efficacious than publishing a book.'

Mrs. Urquhart, with whom the doctor
was evidently a favourite, began to
laugh.

'That is too bad of you, doctor. You
must hear James read his verses some
day; I am not a judge of poetry, but I
think they are remarkable.'

'And I think your judgment infallible,'
said Murdoch, gallantly, to May's secret
amusement. 'Perhaps Mr. Algernon will
read something for us?'

'Algernon is my *nom de plume*,' said the
nephew, modestly. 'My own name is
Robinson, but I am known as the Poet.'

'James Robinson,' Mrs. Urquhart interposed. 'I was at the baptism ; you cried all the time.'

'And no wonder!' May exclaimed. 'I should have cried if I had been victimised in that way. Supposing I were called Robinson!'

'You may come to it yet,' said the doctor, consolingly ; at which May dropped her eyelids and became unconscious, though the poet was speaking.

'It is utterly painful,' he said, 'but one gets used to it. The worst of such names is, that they condemn a man to mediocrity from his birth ; for instance, could Burns ever have been a Jones?'

'I have heard of Burne-Jones,' Murdoch said, flippantly. His remark fell flat before the poet's cool drawl.

'All my energies have been spent in annulling the prophecy of my name.'

'It is given to few men to enjoy such

success,' the doctor said, quickly. 'But
the subject is an interesting one. Do you
notice that names owe their character to
the vowel sound in them?—*a* is open and
fearless; *i* bright and sunshiny; *e* deceitful;
o and *u* dark, bad-tempered, murderous!'

'You condemn yourself!' May cried, merrily. 'Murdoch is terribly dark and murderous! I would rather call you Bonnie
Dundee . . . But what have I said? Why do
you look at me so strangely, Dr. Murdoch?'

She stopped and stared at him, for he
had changed colour and looked blue and
cold.

'Oh, nothing!' he said, shrugging his
shoulders, and laughing. 'Some one
passed over my grave, I think. Humph!
Murdoch is something like murder, as you
say. I am a doctor, you know. And that reminds me of a good story Dr. Gervase was
telling me. He was driving through a

village and noticed the number of graves in the churchyard. "This must be a very unhealthy place," he said, to the coachman. "Na, na," the fellow said, "only we hae ower mony doctors intil it!"'

Mrs. Urquhart smiled.

'I ought to deny the implication of the story,' she said, pleasantly, 'for I owe my life to my doctor. When are you going to put my gratitude to the test, Dr. Murdoch?'

'Sooner perhaps than you think. I am making a list of favours that I shall ask you to grant in alphabetical order. A is —now what begins with A? By Jove! —yes, Alison Dean, of course! Do you know a girl of that name?'

'No; who is she?'

'I believe she works at the Ward Mill. I saw her to-day for the first time in Arbroath, but I know I have met her somewhere before. She was quite poorly dressed this morning, but the first time I saw her she was dressed like a lady of Queen Anne's times in silk and lace. She is hardly likely to have been to any fancy dress balls, I suppose?'

'Alison Dean!' May exclaimed, scornfully. 'Why, everyone knows her. She has worked for Mr. Carnegie a long time now. You dreamed you saw her, doctor?'

'Not I! But I must find out more about her.'

'I saw you looking at her to-day,' May said, quietly. 'I don't admire her style, but she looks kind. I dare say I should like her. I am sure she is worth knowing.'

'I am not sure she is worth my knowing,' said the doctor, carelessly. 'She looks too healthy to be profitable.'

'How sordid!' May exclaimed; relieved,

she scarcely knew why, at the careless speech.

'I don't think so,' said the poet. 'People of robust physique are not profitable, except to the butcher and the baker. For my part, I think rude health is shocking, and is a mark of uncivilisation.'

He lounged languidly in his chair, his air that of extreme feebleness, and Dr. Murdoch rose in sudden irritation and took leave of Mrs. Urquhart.

'This is not a professional visit, Mrs. Urquhart. I must see you to-morrow.'

'Yes, come in to-morrow. I want to tell you about the Guild.'

'Of course! By the way, let me help forward the Guild by finding you a member for it—this Alison Dean. She is the very girl who would appreciate its help. She looks refined and intellectual, and Mearns says she draws and sings well.

I am sure you would like her to join.'

'Do you often get up such an enthusiasm for a girl you have seen only once
in the street, Dr. Murdoch?' May Lindsay
asked primly, determined to show that she
had no faith in this impossible story of a
mill girl dressed in silks and laces.

The doctor looked up sharply at May's
bitter tone, and her colour rose as she met
his keen astonished eyes. Her glance fell
before his look, but a moment later she
lifted her head and proudly confronted
him; and the doctor withdrew his gaze
with an uncomfortable sensation of having
received an electric shock.

He was not among the number of those
men who believe themselves to be irresistible, and he was uneasy when there
occurred to him a possible explanation of
May's coldness and sudden irony. Was
she already so much interested in him

that his passing admiration of another girl could make her angry? The suspicion of such a thing aroused his dismay—to what complication might it lead if May had already given him her love! He stared at her in such undisguised dismay that May was amused at the success of her little speech.

'What is the matter? Why do you look so at me?' she asked.

The doctor recovered himself with a start.

'What did you say?' he asked, laughing harshly. 'That Murdoch was dark and murderous? Oh, yes! that's very true, I am afraid, for I murder my aspirations almost before they are born. Well, good-afternoon!'

May had half-risen, expecting the customary shake of the hand—a ceremony the doctor had begun to regard with pleasure, as affording an excuse for gentle pressure; but he left the room without touching her fingers, and she sat down again white with mortification at his omission of duty.

'What is the matter, May?' Mrs. Urquhart asked. 'Are you not feeling well?'

'Quite well, thank you,' said May, trying to look unconcerned, while she listened to the murmurs of the poet.

'I am so relieved to find, Miss Lindsay, that you are not one of those physically over-endowed beings. I thought your high spirits were due to robust health, and it is a pleasure to discover that you are susceptible to mental shock. Accept my congratulations!'

'But I can't!' May said, forcing a laugh. 'It was not mental shock, but an eminently prosaic stitch in the side that made me feel queer for a moment.'

'Ah, yes, delicacy of constitution; a beautiful trait. There is a sonnet on it in "Heart Throes."'

Meanwhile, Dr. Murdoch was driving towards a patient in the neighbourhood of the Ward Mill. He stopped in a quiet street, and, alighting, entered the cottage, the door of which had been made for a generation the fittest of whom could not boast the doctor's inches. After a while, he came from an inner room, and stood in the kitchen with his back to the fire gazing quizzically at a young man who, seated on the extreme edge of a chair, had yielded himself up to the possession of a spirit of miserable awkwardness.

'Weel, Jamie,' said the doctor, heartily; 'you hae twa o' the nicest bairns ane can set e'e on, an' a bonnie bit wifie a' to yersel'.'

The young fellow looked up, his face very red, but a gratified smile lurking under his moustache.

'Ay hae ye,' the doctor continued. 'An' noo, Jamie, when you hae ae bairn on your knee, an' the ither on your airm, you'll be a gey happy man, an' needna ask for mair.'

The smile broadened on the face of the proud father, who was staring delightedly at the doctor. Murdoch had left the fire-place, and was now on his way to the door.

'Ay, Jamie,' he said, pausing to look back; 'a gey happy man, an' you'll no be wantin' mair: an' thank the Lord, Jamie, I'm no i' your shoon!'

The doctor bent his tall figure under the

door and disappeared, but his hearty voice was heard outside—

'Guid save us, laddie, fat's adae wi' you?'

A boy stood at the door with a pale, frightened face, that he raised at the doctor's question.

'It's at the Ward Mill,' he said, hoarsely. 'A lassie's been thrown among the wheels an' kilt!'

'Who is it?' the doctor asked, sharply, springing into his trap with a sudden memory of a tall, beautiful girl passing through the gates of the Ward Mill.

'It's juist Alison Dean,' he answered; 'they cried to me to rin for the doctor!'

Dr. Murdoch heard no more. With a pale, set face he was driving furiously towards the mill.

CHAPTER III.

AN ACCIDENT AT THE MILL.

LIFE at the mill was generally as monotonous as the motion of the great wheels that during the hours of work kept up an unceasing roar. Early in the morning the girls resumed their daily tasks, the continuous feeding of the large machines that, as relentless as fate, compelled their constant attention.

Alison and Jeanie and Liz worked together in the same room, and each had charge of a frame on which revolved the spindles that needed almost continual replenishing.

Lacking as it did the unceasing interest of novelty, devoid as it was of the pleasures and graces of life, how sordid and prosaic seemed the existence of the mill-workers! What beauty was there in the dusty rooms where the atmosphere was stifling and close in the summer, and heavy and vitiated in winter? What was there fair and attractive in the monotonous labour of tending the machines? A casual observer would have answered—nothing. Yet humanity cannot be in any spot, however mean and unlovely, without investing the place with the dignity and interest inseparable from the presence of human life; and in the mill were to be found all the features that make up the romance and pathos of life. The unlovely walls of the Ward Mill, like the plain face of a good woman, hid patience, courage, hope; the heroism that lives in brave endurance, and all the truest beauty of life.

On this particular afternoon there were present in the mill, at work in the same room, among many others, five girls, in whose commonplace lives would be enacted a tragedy of passion and wrong that should be ennobled by a rare devotion, and brightened by the romance and beauty of love.

But Tibbie Mearns and Bell Macniel gave no hint of the sorrowful fate awaiting them; and Alison Dean and her two friends worked on unconscious of the part they were destined to play in the tragedy of life.

Alison stood at her frame watching the swift motion of the spindles. They had been newly filled, and she was free for the moment to let her thoughts wander to other subjects, and to think over the approaching marriage of Tibbie Mearns with her sailor lover Jim.

Jeanie was employed in another part of the room, but for some reason or other her machine was not working; and seeing her sister standing idle, Liz crossed over to her.

'Oh, Jeanie, fat wull I dae wi' my finger? I cut it a whilie syne, an' noo it winna stop bleedin'.'

'I'll put my hankie roond it; bide a wee till I get it,' Jeanie said.

And resting her foot on the edge of the frame, she proceeded to bandage the finger.

Suddenly, above the roar of wheels and the clatter of machinery, rang out a wild, despairing scream. It was followed by another and another, and every girl became sick with dread as the cries sounded above the deafening tumult.

Alison, tending her frame, needed but an instant to comprehend the ghastly significance of the cries. 'Some one caught in a machine!' The thought flashed through her mind, and her lips grew white. Who was it? From what part of the large room did those agonising shrieks come? The question was answered by Liz flying down the room, gasping, pale, and scarcely able to speak.

'It's oor Jeanie! Rin! rin, Alison! Her fit's i' the wheel! She's like to dee! Haste ye, Alison! Haste ye!'

The words surged in Alison's ears, bringing with them a memory of Jeanie's sad voice, heard only an hour before:

'Fat wad come to her gin I wis awa'?'

Jeanie in the wheels!—in those merciless, cruel wheels that would tear her tender young limbs as though they were tow? Jeanie in the wheels! Perhaps already dead!   A great sob rose in Alison's throat, and her breath came thick and fast, as though it would strangle her; but she hurried forward with Liz.   Not a moment must be lost in flying to Jeanie's help.

The women were already rushing excitedly to the end of the room; and when Alison reached Jeanie, a shrieking crowd surrounded her.   Among the voices Alison could not distinguish her friends, and her heart stopped beating.

'Fat wad come to her gin I wis awa'?' Had the words been a prophecy of her approaching end?

Trembling in every limb, Alison pushed through the thronging group.   They instinctively made way for her, and, before one minute had passed from the time the first scream startled her, she stood by Jeanie's side.   But in one moment how much can be accomplished!   Jeanie was lying on the floor, her foot in the machine, the wheels grinding and turning as though no palpitating flesh was in their toils. Happily the girl was senseless; but Alison sickened at the sight that met her eyes. Then, with stern resolution, she forced back the deadly sickness that threatened to unnerve her; and springing forward through the knot of shrieking girls, she gained the side of the machine, and stretched out her hand. Slower the wheels revolved, and in another instant they were standing motionless, arrested in their ghastly work of mutilation.

A thrill of relief passed through the hearts of all, and the girls screamed to each other that Alison had slipped the belt and saved Jeanie's limb. As for Alison, she stood there with a smile on her white lips, though her arm, whirled round the wheel in the act of stopping the machine, was hanging helpless and bleeding at her side, and she knew it was broken. She turned to one of the girls:

'Please open that window, Bell; and some one go for a doctor.'

Then she kneeled down beside Jeanie, who was lying deathly still. The news of the accident had already reached the manager. He stooped now, and helped Alison to draw the mangled limb from the frame.

'She kens naething,' he said. 'Puir lassie, I'll juist tak' her oot-bye, an' I'll speer aboot this efter.'

He raised the unconscious girl in his arms and carried her out to the yard, where Alison followed him; while the shifting boy, who had mischievously started the machine and caused the accident, escaped from the mill on the pretext of going for the doctor.

'Who is hurt?' Dr. Murdoch asked, sharply, as he entered the yard.

'The lassie Munro,' Bell cried, and a strange look of relief passed over the doctor's face.

Then it was not Alison Dean who had been killed! Liz was in high hysterics, and he turned quickly to one of the women—

'Here, Mrs. Macintyre, take that girl away home, will you?'

'I'll dae that, doctor, for she stays in the same land wi' me. Come awa', lassie; you'll dae nae guid to Jeanie the noo.'

Mrs. Macintyre led the girl away, and the doctor stooped to examine Jeanie's injuries.

'She must be taken to the Infirmary at once,' he said, looking up.

But at the words Jeanie opened her eyes.

'Na, na, I winna gae there; you maun tak' me to my ain hame. Far's Alison?'

Alison came forward and bent over her, and Jeanie looked up entreatingly,

'Dinna lat them tak' me to the Infirmary, Alison. You'll no let me gae?'

'No,' Alison said, reassuringly.

Then she turned to the doctor.

'She had better be taken home. I will attend to her.'

Her tone of quiet command startled the man. He glanced keenly at her, and said to himself that he was not mistaken: he *had* seen her before, as he thought, for it was the same girl he remembered in the quaint dress of flowered silk, and the dainty lace at her throat.

In the face of her expressed wish he found himself unable to insist upon Jeanie's being taken to the Infirmary. But he was not accustomed to yielding to the whims of his patient's friends, and he was intolerant with himself at finding that this girl could so easily influence him.

'Where does she live?' he asked, not removing his eyes from Alison's quiet face.

'In Well's Close,' she answered. 'She is an orphan. I live on the same flat.'

He felt disappointed at the words. He had half expected to hear that Alison lived in one of the better houses of the town, and was merely experimenting on factory life for a whim. But Well's Close was one of the poorest parts of Arbroath, and her residence there identified her with the class among whom she worked.

'Then, perhaps, you had better go to see to her. That hysterical sister will be of no use,' he said.

In the meantime a stretcher had been brought, and Jeanie was laid upon it; then, noticing Alison's pale face, the doctor turned to her good-naturedly—

'You don't look fit to walk. I will drive you round to the house, and you can make the place ready for her.'

He rapidly gave directions to the men with the stretcher, and, as soon as they had started, he walked with Alison to the dog-cart that was waiting. Mearns got up behind, Alison reached her seat without assistance, the doctor sprang in beside her, took the reins, and started for Well's Close.

They drove down the street in silence, then he turned and spoke to Alison, sitting pale and quiet beside him.

'It was very plucky of you to slip the belt. She would have been killed if it had not been for your presence of mind.'

'Oh, no,' said Alison, smiling bravely, though her lips trembled, 'any of the others would have done the same if they had had my father's example to guide them.'

The doctor glanced at her quickly with a question in his eyes. 'Who was your father?' he was tempted to say, but he changed the question to another.

'Do you know they told me you were killed?'

Alison shuddered.

'I thought Jeanie was dead when I saw her lying so pale and still. Is she very badly injured?'

'I can scarcely tell yet,' he answered, cautiously. 'But it would be better to take her at once to the Infirmary, you know.'

'Yes,' Alison answered, 'but it would break her heart; and Liz and I can nurse her at home.'

'You are not easily knocked up? But

this affair seems to have shaken you un-commonly.'

'I am quite strong,' she said, eagerly; 'but the accident was terrible.'

'Yet, after all, it is wonderful that more accidents do not occur in the mills. This is only the second this year—the other took place a fortnight ago. It was curious: the lad was at work, and suddenly his machine stopped, and he looked to see what was the matter before he knew that it was his own hand in the wheel. The thing was done so quickly he felt nothing.'

'Yes, I can understand that—just now I felt nothing——' She stopped abruptly, and then continued, in an altered tone: 'I know the lad you mean, it was Willie Mearns.'

They had reached Well's Close, and now drew up before the door. Dr. Murdoch jumped out to assist Alison to alight. She gave him her left hand, and alighted with difficulty, and he followed her upstairs to Jeanie's attic, passing on the way Mrs. Macintyre's room, from which came a sound of Liz still sobbing. Inside the attic he stopped, and gave a low whistle at sight of the bed in the wall.

'That won't do,' he said, definitely. 'She must have room to lie comfortably, and she could not stretch out her leg in that place.'

'There is an iron bedstead in my room,' Alison said; 'it might be brought in here, for it is only across the landing.'

'That's a good idea! Let me look at the bed, will you?'

Without hesitation, Alison crossed the floor and opened the door of her room. Murdoch's keen eyes took in every detail of the daintily-clean apartment. Nothing

escaped him—the books on the shelves,
the pictures on the wall, the rose on the
window-sill—he saw them all in his rapid
survey; and he decided that there was
nothing in the room to explain the mystery that surrounded Alison. Still there
was an air of refinement in the homely
details that impressed the picture of the
girl in other surroundings upon his imagination; and there was an added deference
in his manner when he spoke again to
her.

'This bed will do capitally. Can you
help me to move it?—or shall I call Mrs.
Macintyre?'

'It is not heavy to lift, but I could not
do it with one hand.'

'What is the matter with the other?' he
asked quickly.

'I broke it in slipping the belt. I should
have taken the handle to stop the machine

but I did not stay to think. Don't trouble
about it now; it will do when you have
seen to Jeanie.'

By this time Dr. Murdoch was exam-
ining the arm that Alison had kept hidden
under her shawl. He unwrapped the
apron folded round it, and gave a quick,
vexed cry.

'Compound fracture! It must be set before it begins to swell. Why didn't you
tell me of it before?'

He held the beautiful round arm tenderly, and looked at Alison with steady,
angry eyes—vexed that she should have
borne so much pain in silence all this
time.

'It is nothing,' she said bravely, though
her suffering eyes contradicted her lips.
'I can wait till Jeanie is attended to. And
I think she had better be brought in here
—the room is pleasanter than hers—and

she can see the trees and birds and sky
from the window.'

'You will be an invalid yourself. Can
you spare the room?'

'Yes, easily. But I think 1 hear them
coming—please help them to bring her in
here.'

The doctor looked at the girl standing
before him calm, self-controlled and unselfish, and a thrill of admiration greater than
that her beauty had aroused passed through
him. He took off the silk neckerchief he
wore, and hastily improvising a sling he
laid her arm in it, and told her to sit down
while Jeanie was carried in. He went
down the stairs muttering to himself—and
being translated, the mutterings resolved
themselves into—

'By George! What a splendid girl!'

Truth to tell, he was more interested in
Alison than in the patient awaiting him

below. Jeanie was at the door, pale and faint; but, when the doctor came near and steadied the stretcher as they carried her up, she smiled at him.

'Weel,' he said, cheerfully, 'ye're no deid yet, lassie! Deid fowk dinna gang *up* aye, ye ken, an' we're risin' the noo. Bide a wee, and we'll hae ye packed as snug as haddies in a barrel in anither minute.'

A moment after and Jeanie found herself tenderly placed on Alison's bed, with Alison herself bending over her, anxious to be of use. This the doctor would not allow.

'No, no,' he said decidedly. 'Jeanie will do very well as she is. Mrs. Macintyre will stay with her while I get some dressing for the foot. Meanwhile do you come with me, and let me set your arm in Dr. Lindsay's surgery. It will save time and be better for you both.'

CHAPTER IV.

WHO IS ALISON?

ALISON did not think of resisting the doctor's quiet decision; and she preceded him downstairs to the trap, where Mearns sat as grimly taciturn as the sphinx. When they reached Dr. Lindsay's house they saw May standing at the door waiting to be admitted. A flush of surprise rose to her face when she caught side of the occupants of the dogcart, and she scornfully observed the undisguised care with which Dr. Murdoch guarded Alison's descent from the high seat.

'He could not have done more for her if she had been a lady,' she said, perking up her nose disdainfully. She stepped aside as the two came up to the door; but Murdoch's quick words aroused her interest.

'There has been an accident at the mill, and I must set this arm at once. Is your father in?'

May's face became grave.

'He has just gone out. Is she badly hurt?'

'Compound fracture. Will you come and help me?'

May shrank back.

'Oh, I couldn't, Dr. Murdoch! I should faint.'

'Very well. Ask Mrs. Lindsay to step into the surgery a minute, will you?'

He passed on hurriedly, and opened the surgery door for Alison, while May went to inform her mother of the accident. Before his splints and bandages were ready there came a brisk little knock at the door, and Mrs. Lindsay walked in, her air business-like and manly.

'Want my help, Dr. Murdoch? Compound fracture, May tells me. Serious?'

'The bone protrudes considerably—I may have to saw it off,' he said, in a low tone.

'I hope not! Let me look at your arm, my dear. I am Dr. Lindsay's senior partner, and a qualified practitioner, though Dr. Murdoch mocks at my credentials, so you need not be afraid of me.'

Alison was not afraid of the decided little woman, whose movements were so bird-like that Dr. Murdoch called her 'the canary,' and she readily allowed her to examine the injured arm.

'H'm! You look like a woman who

will do everything thoroughly—even to breaking an arm. Now then, doctor, I think we are ready. You'll not need those, I am sure.'

She nodded towards a leather case on the table as she spoke; and Dr. Murdoch left it unopened.

With Mrs. Lindsay's help he returned the bone to its place, applied a plaster, and bandaged the arm. Then he placed it again in the sling, and tied the kerchief round Alison's neck. And the girl submitted quietly; though had she known with what dark deed that same silk kerchief would be afterwards associated no power on earth would have induced her to allow him to use it in her service!

'You are the bravest woman I ever saw, my dear!' said Mrs. Lindsay, when the operation was over and Alison had shown no sign of what she suffered. 'Come and see me when you are better. I must run now. My practice is not extensive enough to make me hard-hearted—these things upset me. I should have more of them. Now, Dr. Murdoch, don't look cynical— you have fainted yourself after an operation. Good-bye, my dear, good-bye!'

Pale as death, but brisk and cheery to the last, the little woman fled from the room. Dr. Murdoch opened the door for her, and then returned to Alison.

'Mrs. Lindsay has any amount of pluck; but you have beaten her to-day. You will have to be very careful not to let the external air get to the seat of the fracture, and you must——'

The doctor was interrupted by a knock at the door, and May entered carrying a little tray with a glass of wine on it.

'I thought this would do your patient good,' she said, timidly, conscious that she

had disappointed Dr. Murdoch in refusing
to help him.

'Of course it will,' he said, pleased at her
thoughtfulness.

'No, don't go away; come in and see
your prescription taken.'

May came forward smiling and blushing.

'I am so sorry for your accident,' she
said to Alison. 'Your arm must be dread-
fully painful.'

'Yes,' Alison gasped, 'it is—rather—
painful.'

She had risen from her chair to speak to
May, and now she staggered, and would
have fallen had not Dr. Murdoch caught
her in his arms.

'May,' he cried, sharply, 'move that
chair, and let me put her on the couch.'

It was the first time he had called her
by her Christian name, and the girl blushed
in happy self-consciousness as she made

way for him to lay his burden on the sofa. He administered restoratives, and Alison soon opened her eyes.

'She will be all right immediately; but I must get away to the other girl. Will you stay with her till I return?'

'Yes, I should like to,' May answered him, in restored good-humour at being made a sharer in his work. He gave her a look that would have been sufficient compensation for a more unpleasant task, and with a passing glance at Alison he hurried away once more. May's jealousy died away under that look, and she exerted herself to justify his confidence in her. She brought eau de Cologne, and bathed Alison's head, and fanned her gently, wondering at the beauty that pain could not dim.

'She is lovely,' May thought, smoothing back the masses of black hair that had been unloosed, and now fell over the carpet in a dark, rippling luxuriance. 'She is lovely, and quite a lady. I dare-say he *has* seen her beautifully dressed somewhere, for she does not look like a factory girl. I should like to know her history. I could almost be jealous of her; but now I know that he likes me, for he never called me " May " before. Of course, Dr. Murdoch would never marry a factory girl, though she was ever so pretty!'

'I am afraid I am giving you a lot of trouble,' said Alison, interrupting her thoughts.

'Oh, not at all. Do you feel any better? You fainted, you know.'

'Yes, I thought of Jeanie. Her foot was in the horrible, crushing wheels—I can hear them now.'

She covered her face shuddering, and May asked hoarsely:

'Jeanie? Was she killed?'

'No; the machine was stopped in time. Am I keeping the doctor from her?'

'No; he has gone. You are in my charge. Let me give you some wine now.'

'No, thank you. I must go back to Jeanie.'

'Not till Dr. Murdoch returns. He told me to keep you, and I always obey him.'

She blushed meaningly, and into her whole appearance there came an air of conscious appropriation of the doctor. She cast a sidelong glance at Alison, to see if she had accepted the significance of her air and words, but Alison had noticed neither.

'He is very kind and thoughtful,' she said, wearily; 'he has been very good to me to-day.'

'He is good to everybody who is poor and needy,' said May; feeling as though she gave expression to a pious sentiment, though she was only impressing Alison with the idea that the doctor's attentions had been called forth by her poverty and destitution, and were therefore of no value.

Alison closed her eyes wearily and made no reply.

'Excuse me,' said May, after a while. 'Will you tell me how it is you are different from the other mill-girls? Your accent is English, and you are not as rough as some of them.'

Alison flushed at this disrespect to her friends.

'My parents were English; I have not always worked at the mill.'

'Oh,' May cried, eagerly, 'do tell me if you ever wore anything different from the gown you have on. Used you to wear silk dresses and lace and pretty things?'

A red flush rose to the girl's face, and she was crimson from chin to brow as she turned away from May's curious eyes.

'I have worn such things,' she said, very quietly. The still reserve of the reply checked May from further questioning; and she remained silent until the sound of wheels drew her to the window.

'That is Dr. Murdoch, I know; he drives so quickly that father is always telling him he will be upset and killed some day. Yes, he is coming in! Before he comes, do tell me who you are; I want to know really very much.'

'I am Alison Dean of the Ward Mill,' Alison answered proudly, as Dr. Murdoch entered.

He crossed to the sofa at once.

'How is Jeanie?' Alison cried, eagerly;

glad to turn away from May's baffled eyes.

'I left her sleeping. You must keep her very quiet, and take care of yourself at the same time. Are you feeling better? Got over the faintness?'

'Yes, thank you,' Alison said, rising to go.

And then her eyes drooped, and her face crimsoned, and she stood before him in a beautiful confusion, for the heavy wealth of her hair had escaped from its fastening and veiled her from head to foot in soft black waves. It fell all round her, hiding her short skirts and ugly bodice, and nearly touched the ground in its wonderful abundance; and the doctor stood in bashful wonder at her lovely consciousness. He had never seen anything so beautiful as this girl, with her veiled eyes and crimson cheeks, drooping under the cloud of her own loveliness; but he laughed away the embarrassment of the situation.

'You'll want both your arms to manage all those ebon locks. Was it Medusa whose hair was all serpents? I must run away before I am turned to stone. I'll be in to see you and Jeanie to-morrow.'

He went hurriedly from the room, and Alison looked at May with a deprecating air.

'How stupid of me not to know my hair was loose! And now I cannot put it up with my left arm.'

'Let me do it,' said May, kindly: 'You roll it into a great bob, don't you? How lovely it is! I never saw such hair.'

She twisted the great masses round Alison's head, and pinned on her shawl for her in her kindest manner.

'There! you are all right now. I hope

you will soon be better. I must come in to see you and Jeanie.'

'Thank you,' said Alison, soberly, passing into the hall where Dr. Murdoch was standing.

'You are not able to walk, so Mearns will drive you home. Remember to be careful of your arm.'

He opened the door for her, and helped her into the trap, and then returned to May, who was watching him from the surgery window.

'Dr. Murdoch, she is lovely!' May exclaimed, enthusiastically, as soon as he came in.

'Is she?' the doctor asked, drily. 'She is not as beautiful as she is brave!'

And May, pondering over his words, comforted herself—as little girls will who know nothing of the complex nature of the animal, man—by saying he could not

have been so struck with her beauty since
he preferred her bravery to it. She ran
upstairs, lightly humming a little snatch
of song :

> 'There are three kisses that I call to mind,
> And I will sing their praises as I go ;
> The first, a kiss too courteous to be kind,
> Was such a kiss as monks and maidens know ;
> As sharp as frost, as blameless as the snow.'

A cynical smile curled the doctor's lips,
and as he heard the gay little ditty floating up the stairs, he said to himself—
and surely the quotation must have been
irrelevant—

> 'As moonlight unto sunlight, and as
> water unto wine.'

May's little figure disappeared from
view, and at the same time passed from
Murdoch's thoughts, banished for the time
being by the lovely vision of Alison as she
had stood with burning cheeks and her
hair all about her. After all, he was only

a young man, and a young man with a very healthy admiration for, and interest in, the opposite sex. He did not, as so many of his own age, regard woman as an unfledged angel. He knew too much about her for such a pretty illusion to be possible ; but experience taught him that woman's influence was the most important factor in human life, and he kept his eyes open that he might be able to recognize the woman who should rule his own life.

Had he met her?

A week ago he would scarcely have hesitated to reply in the affirmative. Destiny pointed to May Lindsay as his future wife, and he had not contested her fiat. To-day, with the uncertainty of love, he shrank from the 'yes' that his heart would fain have uttered.

'After all,' he soliloquised, 'I have never been in love yet; and I am not going to marry a girl merely because she has beautiful hair and more character than most women. Character in a wife may be a very uncomfortable thing. It's less risky to marry one of those little clinging women, whose mind is all conviction that her husband is perfect. It answers in the long run ; and mental inanity is better than intellectual pugnacity. Yet what a blessing that determined little woman has been to Lindsay—quite the making of him ! On the other hand, look at Gervase—his wife puts him in her pocket, poor wretch ! Mrs. Murdoch's husband ? By George, not if I know it ! Thank Heaven, I am heart-whole !'

But that evening he walked down the street with erect head, through the glare of the shops and the bustle of the pavement ; and there was a proud light in his eyes as he muttered to himself some lines

that were surely inappropriate to the
severely practical aspects of the shop-
windows and gas-lamps :

> '"To-day the world to me has grown so fair
>   I dare not trust myself to think of it ;
>   Visions of light around me seem to flit,
> And Phœbus loosens all his golden hair
>   Right down the sky ; and daisies turn and stare
>   At things we see not with our common wit." '

Mrs. Lindsay's maid, following the doctor
down the street, caught here and there a
word of this soliloquy.

'He was haverin' awfu', Miss May,' she
reported afterwards ; 'an' a' I heard wis
somethin' aboot gowden hair.'

'*Golden* hair, Mary? Are you *sure* it
was not raven hair, or dark hair? Are
you quite, quite certain it was golden
hair?' May asked, excitedly.

'Quite certain, miss ; it was juist gowden
hair, an' naethin' else.'

And May, standing before the glass that
evening, smiled at the locks, less abundant

but brighter than Alison's, that fell around her in a golden shower. Poor, foolish little May! Of such fine strands is made the web that holds a woman's heart.

Meanwhile the doctor went on his way, unconscious that he had been speaking aloud. He paused under the pend as eight o'clock rang out from the old church, and then hurried his steps, for he had still several patients to see that night.

In a dark side street he paused before a door; his hand, seeking the latch, arrested by a clear, high voice that came floating out into the darkness. Full yet piercing, it seemed to fill the silence with sound as a rose fills a room with sweetness; and he waited outside to listen. Air and words were both well-known to him: they belonged to one of the dear old songs that never lose their pathos and melody, and he listened with a Scotchman's keen enjoyment of familiar music:

'Unhook the west port and let us gae free,
    For it's up wi' the bonnets o' Bonnie Dundee.'

'Humph!' said the doctor, smiling. 'May Lindsay called me Bonnie Dundee to-day; but if the girl singing is Alison Dean, she has more claim to the title than I have.'

'Ye hae no seen the last o' my bonnets and me!'

Alison's song came to an end, and Murdoch found himself trembling with an excitement he would, in another, have called loss of tone. Her voice had moved him unaccountably, and he had to stop and ridicule his folly before common-sense asserted itself, and he was composed enough to open the door and go in. There sat Alison, as he had expected, deathly white, by the side of little Willie Mearns. At sight of her evident suffering the doctor lost his excitement and became purely professional.

'It is utter madness for you to be out

to-night,' he said, hastily. 'Didn't you understand that I prescribed bed and quiet for you?'

Alison looked with surprise at his angry face.

'Yes,' she said quietly, 'but I had promised to come in and sing to Willie, and I always keep my word.'

'Fiddlesticks! Much better keep your bed. That and a secret seem to be two of the things no woman can keep. Go home now, and in future allow me to keep your word for you!'

'Ah, no, doctor! It is as much as you can do to keep your temper. I will not burden you with anything of mine.'

Alison's merry eyes and pretty smile were irresistible. Murdoch could not resent the words, and he sat down laughing.

'Eh? What's that you say? Well, you must own I have good reason to be cross.

I don't want you to be laid up, heaven knows how long. You must really be careful of yourself.'

'I shall be obedient after this,' Alison said wearily, losing the colour her retort had called into her cheek. 'Good-night, Willie—you will not expect me for a while. Good-night, Dr. Murdoch.'

'Stay,' said the doctor. 'I have to see a patient in your neighbourhood and I may as well go with you.'   Alas! so far had this honourable young man fallen from the truth that he congratulated himself on his readiness of resource even while he sacrificed his veracity to the wish to talk to Alison. The girl barely acknowledged the courtesy. Excitement had increased the pain in her arm, and she was glad to get into the air from the close atmosphere of the cottage.

During the walk to Well's Close the doctor hovered near the subject closest to his heart. When had he seen Alison before? But though he tried to introduce the subject, she seemed bent on avoiding it. He could not ask her directly; and when he had parted from her he assured himself that his interest in her was at an end. But he must have deceived himself in this. How else can it be accounted for that all night he was haunted by a pale, beautiful face and sweet, beseeching eyes framed in a twilight of dusky hair? How is it that through all his dreams ran a wild pathetic voice that was not May Lindsay's? And what was the song?

'Then each cavalier who loves honour and me,
Let him follow the bonnets o' Bonnie Dundee!'

CHAPTER V.

HER HERO.

Dr. Murdoch was stepping quickly along the pavement, so intent on his own thoughts that he had no recognition for the people he met or passed in the street. He was going from Well's Close, and he found that, so far from Alison having lost interest for him, further association with her had only deepened the impression she had made at first.

It was in vain that he mocked at himself, and spoke scornfully of his infatuation; his interest in the girl was too strong to be overwhelmed by scorn or mockery. Yet it was positively ludicrous that he should be so persistently haunted by a girl of whose existence he had been unconscious a fortnight ago.

It was not a novel thing for him to develop a sudden interest in the girls he met in society. But that was altogether a different thing from this, he said, using his favourite quotation, as 'moonlight unto sunlight,' &c. Attention to the fair was a duty, and if the performance of duty was not rewarded by interest given and provoked, well, then—he shrugged his shoulders carelessly—duty was its own reward!

He was not unduly self-assertive; and, indeed, under his frank and kindly exterior there was a shyness and humility that few suspected. He was a wholesome, manly fellow; a brother of whom sisters are proud, a man whom women instinctively trust. He had flitted through several seasons in Arbroath, and had learned the useful art of bestowing his attentions on ladies with so fine an impartiality that they could bear a mathematical test, and be found exactly proportioned to each. The result of this was that he had been reported engaged to each in turn of all the marriageable ladies of the town and neighbourhood.

May Lindsay was the latest victim to his sense of justice; but when he was congratulated on his engagement, the doctor disavowed all intentions of marrying; while Dr. Lindsay, being appealed to, sought refuge in a general statement to the effect that Dr. Murdoch would marry everybody if he could!

Murdoch was a great anxiety to the

matrons of the district. It was not good for man to be alone, they said; especially in a large, well-furnished house like the doctor's! And the younger ladies became tenderly solicitous for his health, and wondered if his housekeeper warmed his slippers and gave him hot drinks when he came home cold and wet from his long journeys. Occasionally these feminine murmurs penetrated to the doctor's ears, and then, in an access of gratitude for such consideration, he would declare that Dr. Lindsay was right, and he should like to marry them all!

Dr. Murdoch began now to distrust his philanthropy, and to see in it a weak and unmanly avoidance of the duty of concentrating his affections on one only.

'After all,' he had said, with quiet cynicism, ' the success of marriage depends on a man's faculty for discovering happiness in adverse conditions—for accepting the half as more than the whole.'

But his pet theory was this:—Given two people deaf, dumb, and blind, and you have the only reliable conditions of domestic felicity! Like the views strongly held by those they do not affect in practice, this theory answered well enough for him so long as he was not personally interested in it. But now he began to question whether there might not be truth in those worn-out and unadapted-to-present-experience notions of the necessity of harmony in thought and aim in the married life ; and especially in that ridiculous, old, exploded idea of affection between husband and wife.

When a man begins to question the truth of a principle that has long existed undisputed, we may fairly conclude that he wishes to prove it unsafe. He had been attending Alison and Jeanie for a fortnight, and his visits to them had become the event of his day. Both girls needed constant attention, especially Alison, for the doctor could not entrust the dressing of her arm to anyone but himself. He said professional skill was required in removing the bandages; and as he was an accredited practitioner, no one disputed the statement.

He was anxious about Jeanie, and had begun to fear that it would be necessary to amputate the limb; but he said nothing of his anxiety, and would talk cheerfully to her when Alison was present. In Alison's absence it must be confessed that he said little, and that little only what was necessary to keep Jeanie talking about her friend. In this way he became acquainted with all of the girl's history that Jeanie knew ; but the mystery he associated with her still remained unexplained.

Alison was prevented from going to the mill by her accident, so she spent a great part of the day in reading and singing to the invalid ; and sometimes the doctor would arrive during the singing, and would stay outside listening to the sweet voice that changed the hours of pain into seasons of deepest enjoyment. When Alison sang he told himself that it was her beautiful voice that charmed him. When the song was over, he found her silence more charming than her music.

'Miss Alison,' he said to her one day, 'you will not return to the mill when your arm is strong again ?'

'I must,' Alison said, brightly. 'How else shall I live ?'

'There are plenty of more suitable occu-

pations for you. Factory-work is not fit
for you; don't you feel that?'

'No,' she returned. 'No work is unfit
for us; all honest labour is honourable.'

'That's just Alison,' Liz said, impatiently.
'She's aye crackin' aboot fat she ca's the
dignity o' wark. I'd like weel eneuch to
dae withoot such dignity gin I could!'

The doctor smiled.

'The dignity of work, eh? Whose
phrase is that, Miss Alison?'

'I am not sure. I think Carlyle adopted
it from Goethe.'

Dr. Murdoch raised his eyebrows.

'Do you read Carlyle?'

'Yes; I have just finished *Heroes and
Hero-Worship.*'

'And who is your favourite hero?'

'My father,' she said, proudly. 'I wish
you had known him; he was brave and

gentle and strong, and he died so nobly. He gave up his place in the boat to a dying man. Father would not leave him on board; and he put him in the boat while he remained behind and went down with the ship. The poor man died before the boat's crew was picked up.'

'It was a noble deed,' he said; and he looked away from Alison's bright eyes and kindling cheeks to the book-case on the wall.

'Are all those books yours?'

'No, some are borrowed.'

'Ay,' Liz interrupted. 'Alison has a freend that len's her mony a bookie, Andra' Rayne, the hackler. He's awfu' ta'en up wi' her, an' Alison's just as ta'en up wi' him.'

A faint colour came into Alison's cheek.

'He is very clever, and all the hacklers read a great deal. They lend each other books, and Andra' gives me a sight of them.'

'That's right,' said the doctor, heartily. 'I know this Rayne. Didn't he once publish some poems?'

'Yes, but he was very young,' Alison said, deprecatingly.

Dr. Murdoch laughed.

'Oh, that's very true! We must be very young to publish our verses now-a-days. Happily I have passed the epoch without committing myself to print.'

'Do you write poetry?' Alison asked.

It was the first time she had shown any interest in his pursuits, and the doctor was gratified.

'No; but I'm not one of those people who couldn't write a line to save their lives. I can write *one* line; it is when it comes to two that I am beaten! If you are fond of poetry I will lend you some of the moderns. Who is your favourite poet?'

'Spenser,' she answered.

'Noo, then, Alison,' Liz cried, saucily. 'I wis thinkin' it has been Andra' these twa years at ony rate.'

' You are a daft lassie,' Alison said, laughing, but the doctor noticed the red flush that covered her face with a pretty confusion. Somehow he did not like the bright colour, and he rose hastily.

' Well, good-day,' he said, abruptly.

And the girls heard his boots clattering with unnecessary vehemence down the wooden stair. He bent his steps towards the Abbey, for he was going to visit Mrs. Urquhart, whose house adjoined it. The Abbey house was south of the great pile, and had once been the Abbot's house. Originally it was a square tower, the basement floor of which was a large kitchen with groined arches and pillars, still in fine preservation ; but the tower had been replaced by a dwelling-house, and in this Mrs. Urquhart lived. She received the doctor with more than her usual warmth of welcome, her fine eyes lighting up as she shook hands with him.

'I've been wanting you all day, doctor. Can you help me in a difficulty ?'

'Depends what it is. If you are seriously ill I can have a consultation with Mrs. Lindsay.'

'No, no, it's not myself. It's the Guild.'

'Oh, Mrs. Urquhart, that Guild will be the death of you yet! It's a disease that baffles my skill. Even Mrs. Lindsay would refuse to diagnose it. What is wrong now ?'

'Everything, everything ! Just when

the hall is built, and we are ready to start, it has to be given up.'

'Of course; what I expected. Women shouldn't ride hobbies, they are certain to be thrown in time. What do you want me to do?'

'Make me well in a fortnight.'

'Ah, that is beyond me! You must go to an advertising quack if you wish to be cured by telegram.'

Mrs. Urquhart laughed. She and the doctor were on the best of terms. When he came a stranger to Arbroath she had been very kind to him, but until of late he had submitted to rather than appreciated her kindness.

He had a young man's intolerance of feminine enthusiasm and emotional fervour —two strong characteristics of Mrs. Urquhart—and it had annoyed him to see a woman of her years—she was over fifty—

putting her finger into all the social and philanthropic pies of Arbroath life.

The doctor's philosophy of woman's work did not include efforts for others, and did not extend beyond the sphere of narrowed home life. The whole duty of young ladies, he said, was to be pretty and entertaining to man: of matrons—to conduct their households and give good dinners; of elderly ladies—to grow old gracefully, and, as chaperons, to be blind and deaf. But Mrs. Urquhart found work for herself in other directions. She was trying to establish a Guild for the mill girls of Arbroath, that would be a home to the homeless, and supply healthy recreation to those who had homes of their own.

A hall had been built in the centre of the town, with reading-rooms and every facility for classes of study, cookery, and art. The girls had contributed as much

as would pay the current expenses; but
when everything was ready, Mrs. Urquhart had met with an accident that put
a stop to all her plans. For weeks she
hovered between life and death, and, when
at last she returned to life, it was to be a
helpless cripple for the rest of her days.
When Murdoch saw the quiet heroism and
courage with which she accepted her sad
lot, and the patient endurance with which
she gathered up the fragments of her life,
determined to use them to the best purpose, he gave her a sympathy and admiration as unstinting as his dislike had been
ill-founded. They became fast friends, and
she found her warmest coadjutor in him.

'I want to be well in a fortnight,' she
said. 'If something is not done immediately, the whole thing will fall through.
It is certain to fail unless some capable
person will take the direction of it.'

'I thought Mrs. Lindsay was director?'

'Mrs. Lindsay? She is as innocent of
direction as the flea Marget was trying
to catch this morning! Unpaid labour,
whether in committees or in trade, is
always unreliable. Now, if I could find a
woman with a genius for management, I
would give her a good salary merely to
carry out my wishes. I'd do away with
Mrs. Lindsay and her staff—it is impossible for professional ladies to be philanthropic—and take the direction into my
own hands. What do you think of my
idea?'

'It is capital! And I think I know the
very woman you want.'

Mrs. Urquhart lifted up her hands
despairingly.

'Now, don't say any more. I know you
are going to propose Alison Dean. Since
you have been attending her you can

talk of no one else; its really disgraceful.'

He took no notice of the charge.

'She is just the girl for you—splendidly suited for what you want.'

'I wish you would be serious, doctor. I want a woman of culture and refinement to influence the girls, not a mill-hand, one of themselves !'

'By birth she is a lady,' he said, eagerly. 'A refined—a beautiful woman——'

'Oh, have you found out that she has not always been in the mill? Is it true that you met her before?' Mrs. Urquhart interrupted.

The doctor's face became red, and he looked confused.

'No, I can't tell,' he stammered. 'I couldn't ask her pointedly, you know. But she is a lady; and as for culture, she reads Spenser and quotes Carlyle and Goethe: If you heard her sing, or saw her only, you would not hesitate as to her suitability for the Guild.'

'Well, I think I must take your word for it. And I will ask her to call, that I may judge for myself. I will send for her to-morrow. I wonder now—if she is so beautiful as you say, and reads and sings well—there is no knowing—I might like her to live here. Why, there's even a possibility I might adopt her. James is provided for already, and she is an orphan. There's no knowing. By the way, what do you think of James, Dr. Murdoch?'

The doctor had risen to go. For some unaccountable reason his face was radiant; and he looked very boyish and handsome as he shook hands with Mrs. Urquhart.

'What do I think of him?' he said, gaily. 'Oh, he would have been hatched a genius, only the egg was addled!'

CHAPTER VI.

JEANIE'S LOVE.

JEANIE, poor girl, lay watching Alison, her face pale and suffering, for the pain in her crushed limb was now almost constant. She could not understand it, nor did she suspect the anxiety with which Dr. Murdoch was watching the case. The doctor was doing his best to save the limb, but Mrs. Lindsay, who considered herself a specialist in surgery, gave him no hope that he would do this. She often came in to see the girls, for she had taken a fancy

to Alison, and her cheery presence was a
great relief to the monotony of the sick
room. May, too, was a frequent visitor;
but Liz resented the patronage of her
visits, and the small presents she brought
the two invalids; for May took pains to
show that Liz had no share in her
bounty.

'She's no bonnie,' Liz said, 'an' I'm no
carin' for her comin' to speer at oor Jeanie
aboot the doctor. I ken he thinks a sicht
mair o' my face than o' hers! You should
rise, Jeanie, an' gang oot bye whenever
you hear her comin' up the stair.'

Jeanie only smiled sadly, thinking how
happy she would be if she were able to
rise at all. She was becoming used now
to lying in Alison's bed opposite the window, through which she could see the
clouds drifting across the sky. And there,
shut in by her pain, she found strength as

she learned from nature the peace that lies
at the heart of all beauty.

Her only field of view was a few square
feet of sky, across which rose the branches
of the lilac tree; yet in that narrow space
Nature revealed herself and spoke to
Jeanie. New thoughts, roused by this
deep-toned voice, woke in her; and shadow
and cloud and stormy wind sweeping
across the spaces of her vision became the
characters of a new language of wonderful
meaning. The lilac tree especially was an
endless source of amusement and interest.
It is true the branches were bare, but they
were haunted by a robin that everyday
chirped cheerily from the boughs, and at
night slept safely folded in the snuggest
fork of the tree. The sparrows, too, were
busy in it during the day; and when the
darkness hushed their chirping and the
robin's song, the tree had still a voice, for

a star shone through its branches—a song of light in the silence of the darkness.

It was well for Jeanie that she could find interest in these things, for the days were long and weary, and many times she had to struggle against the tears it distressed Alison to see. Unselfishness and a passionate love for Alison were the first fruits of her discipline of pain; and Jeanie in suffering was learning the great truth that all advance in character is the outcome of struggle and the result of trial.

The girls had grave talks about Liz, and often the tears that Jeanie would not shed for her own pain flowed unchecked on her sister's account. Liz was very pretty, and much admiration was turning her foolish little head; and Jeanie, who knew the temptations and dangers of factory life, was full of anxiety for her sister's future. Alison had great influence over her; but since the accident Liz had become intimate with Bell Macniel, who belonged to a wild set, and did the girl no good, and Alison feared that she would lose her hold on her. But she had such pretty ways that, when she came coaxing, Alison could not withstand her; and many a time did she shield Liz from Jeanie's anger, and help her out of the scrapes into which her high spirits led her. Liz meanwhile took all this as a a matter of course, and never looked forward to the future with the dark cloud hanging over her, when she would requite Alison's love with ingratitude and bitter pain.

'I think whiles, Alison,' Jeanie said, one day, 'if Liz was merried, I would dee in peace.'

'Toots! Who is to marry a child like that? She's but a lassie yet.'

'Ay; but, Alison, it gars me greet when I mind how saucy-like she is wi' the lads. Fat would she dae gin I was to dee?'

'Jeanie! I'll not listen to you talking like that. You're not going to die yet; and it's silly to trouble about Liz—girls are always giddy when they're young. You might as well say Liz is in love with the doctor because she answers him when he teases her.'

'She was ower daft wi' him yon day. Dae ye mind, Alison, fat she was sayin' to him aboot Andra' an' you?'

'Ay,' Alison answered, shortly. 'It's a good thing Andrew didn't hear her.'

'Was she richt, Alison?' Jeanie asked, wistfully. 'Are you awfu' fond o' Andra'?'

'I don't know,' Alison said, gazing

absently beyond Jeanie. 'What makes you ask?'

There was no answer, and Alison looked questioningly at her friend.

'Dinna speer at me!' Jeanie cried, seeing the glance; and then, to Alison's dismay, she burst into tears.

Alison crossed the room hurriedly, and knelt down by the bed, putting her cheek tenderly against Jeanie's pale face.

'Hush, hush, lassie! Don't cry so. What is it now?'

The kind voice was too much for Jeanie. She threw her arms round Alison's neck, and hid her face on her bosom while she sobbed out:

'Oh, Alison, Alison! I'll never get better gin Andra' disna lo'e me!'

A sharp pang went through Alison at the words; but she only drew the trembling

girl closer to her ; and her voice was steady
as she asked,

'Do you love him then, Jeanie, so
much ?'

'Ay, do I,' she sobbed. 'Oh, Alison, I
hae aye loved him, an' I didna think 'twas
you he liked till Liz spoke o' him an'
you to the doctor. An, noo, gin she spak
true I wad dee, for I cannot leeve withoot
him.'

The great moments of life come and go,
and no voice whispers to us that they are
potent for the future. We pass them by,
not knowing that they have opened doors
into a destiny that no hand can ever close
again. Such a moment had come to
Alison, and she was unaware of its de-
finiteness.

Alison knelt with her cheek pressed to
Jeanie's, and trembled under a conflict

between friendship and love. She knew
in her heart that Liz was right—she knew
that Andrew Rayne loved her—and she?
She could not deny her own feeling for
him—yes, she loved him in return. She
owed most of her intellectual and artistic
life to him: and it was not strange that his
influence, which had touched her at the
points of art and intellect, should also have
reached the seat of the emotions.

The recognition of beauty not only opens
the avenues to new views of the beautiful;
it arouses a beauty in ourselves, a beauty
that we call love. And this love Alison
owed to Rayne, who had touched her eyes
and enabled her to see the fairness and
beauty of life. Was she to renounce
his love for the whim of a sick girl? Even
if Jeanie's life hung on her decision, was it
right that she should let her cherish a
fruitless hope? And if Jeanie were to

die, her renunciation would be a useless
sacrifice.

Alison remained silent; and in the
silence she remembered the story she had
told Dr. Murdoch, of her father's heroic
surrender of life for a man whose hours
were numbered. He had unhesitatingly
given his life for a dying man; and she,
who professed to take up this noble father's
principles, could not bear to renounce a
mere joy to purchase another's life.

'Say he doesna lo'e you, Alison,' Jeanie
pleaded.

Alison raised her eyes; they fell on a
book lying open on the bed, and half-uncon-
sciously she read the words—

'*If we love those we lose, we cannot altogether lose those we love.*'

She caught her breath quickly, then she
whispered,

'Hush, Jeanie! Andrew has never told

me he loved me, and I have only a sister's love to give him.'

She trembled as she said the words; but instead of a dumb despair, she felt a quiet that was surely the blessedness of self-surrender, when Jeanie answered,

'Oh! I'm glad o' that, Alison. I would hae deid gin you had said you lo'ed him.'

Alison rose as there came a tap at the door. It was May Lindsay with a pretty colour in her face, and a pretty smile on her lips, fresh and bright from an interview with Dr. Murdoch. She was followed by Liz, who came from her work for dinner, and the two girls looked at each other as rival beauties might; only that the pride in Liz's glance was more contemptuous than the disdain in May's.

'Well, Jeanie,' May said, brightly, 'are you feeling stronger to-day? and is your arm better, Alison?'

Not waiting for a reply to either question, she went on gaily—

'See, I have brought you some eggs—really new-laid they are. And what book have you been reading, Alison?'

She had caught sight of the volume on the bed, and now she put two eggs on the table, and took up the book.

'Thackeray!' she exclaimed. 'Do you girls read books like this? Where did you get the book, Alison?'

Sweet-tempered as she was, Alison resented the roughness and curiosity of the girl, and showed it by not soon replying to the question. But Liz was ready enough with her tongue, and she answered May.

'Na,' she said, roughly: '*girls* dinna read books like yon, but oor Alison is a leddy, an' there's ane that kens it better than such as you, an' he lends her books.'

'Liz!' Alison exclaimed, admonishingly.

But the shaft had sped home, and with red cheeks May was turning over the pages of the book.

'John Murdoch,' she read. 'Is it Dr. Murdoch's?'

'Ay, is it,' Liz answered; 'an' Alison kens hoo to speak wi' him aboot a' the fowk that's in it.'

At this moment there was another rap at the door, and Liz broke off in her speech, and hurriedly threw her apron over the eggs on the table. At her invitation to enter, Mrs. Urquhart's Marget came in with a note for Alison, which she delivered in grim silence and retired. As soon as the door closed upon her, Liz took her apron from the eggs, and said to May, with a gleam of spiteful humour in her eye,

'I didna wish her to see that you had only brocht twa, you ken!'

May was dying with curiosity to know the contents of the note, but this thrust was too much for her. Summoning all her dignity to her aid she took leave of Jeanie and Alison, with a fine unconsciousness of any other presence in the room, and calmly retired from the scene of conflict. But as soon as she reached the street her dignity forsook her, and she stamped her foot angrily, with a muttered—

'So he lends her books, and thinks she is a lady! Very well, Dr. Murdoch! But if you imagine you are going to throw me over for Alison Dean you will find yourself mistaken!'

Meanwhile Alison was reading aloud Mrs. Urquhart's note.

'"Mrs. Urquhart will be obliged to Alison Dean if she will take the trouble to call at the Abbey House to-day, at three o'clock." I wonder what she wants me for!'

Jeanie looked up eagerly.

'Oh, Alison, dinna you ken? She has heard o' the way you stoppit the machine, an' she wad speer at you aboot it. She's an awfu' wifie, aye fashin' hersel' wi' the lassies. Wull you gang, Alison?'

'Surely,' Alison said. 'Perhaps she wishes to ask after you—she is sick herself, you know, poor lady.'

'Na, na,' Liz said. 'It's yersel' she wants to see. But it's gone twa the noo, an' you canna gang i' that gown. Come awa' and let me gie you a han' in shiftin' it.'

Alison, with a rueful glance at her arm, submitted; and Liz soon transformed her from a pretty mill-girl into a beautiful woman.

In her short skirt, with the tartan shawl over her head, Alison looked very different from what she did now in her gown of

dark tweed and jaunty little hat with the
red wing in it. Liz regarded her with
envious admiration; and Jeanie raised
herself in bed to take in the full effect of
this unwonted elegance.

'Ye're juist fine, Alison,' she said. 'You
look awfu' weel, only a wee bittie pale.'

'Ay,' said Liz, 'an' there isna a leddy
amang them a' sae bonny. I wish yon
prood lass, May Lindsay, micht hae a
sicht o' you noo, sae I dae!'

Alison laughed.

'There is nothing very bonny in this
ugly black sling; it spoils everything.'

'You should tak the doctor's hankie he
gied you yon time; it's white, an' a gey
sicht bonnier than that,' Liz said. 'Bide
a wee, Alison, I ken far it is, an' I'll seek
it presently.'

'No, no, Liz, I am not to use that again.
I'll go just now; so good-bye, Jeanie.'

She nodded brightly, and tripped down the steps with light feet, for there was a pleasant excitement about this visit to the Abbey House.

Dr. Murdoch had told her about Mrs. Urquhart and her Guild, and that suggestion about his neckerchief had recalled him to her mind. He had been very kind and attentive since the day of the accident, but she was thinking more of his bluntness and honesty than of his goodness.

' Goodness,' Alison said to herself, with the generalisation of inexperience, ' is a very commonplace virtue. But, as the doctor says, an honest man is almost as rare as a truthful ecclesiastic.'

Then she laughed at herself for remembering that cynical remark of Dr. Murdoch ; and, looking up as she crossed the street, she met his eyes fixed upon her. She bowed in some confusion, blushing beautifully at being detected in the act of thinking about him, and she shot a swift glance at him to see if he detected her embarrassment.

This he had not done. All he had seen was the graceful and high-bred air of this girl who so irresistibly influenced him. He passed on with a glow on his cheek; and there faded from his memory the picture of that girl in the flowered silk and costly lace. Even the gipsy face under the glorious hair became dim in the light of this last vision of a fair, gracious woman, and a pretty head crowned by a demure little hat with a red wing in it.

'No other woman shall be my wife!' he said to himself, definitely; unconscious, happily, that destiny had united all its forces to prevent this consummation so devoutly to be wished.

'No other woman shall be my wife,' he

said, and yet, in a few months, he would be engaged to another woman! What sports of fate and fortune are we, after all!

CHAPTER VII.

IN THE ABBEY.

THREE o'clock had not yet struck, and Alison went into the Abbey until it should be time to keep her appointment; and also she wanted to see Alec, the curator, who was one of her friends.

The little man was a character, though there was nothing in his appearance to denote it, for he was much under the middle size, and was so thin that Mrs. Urquhart's maid said she could see through him. Wiser people than Marget had failed to do that; but Alec's dry, pawky humour, racy stories, and tales of old superstitions made him a general favourite. He had a reputation for pulling the long bow; but as he never expected his listeners to go the whole length with him—unless they were English tourists, who accepted and paid for the impossible—his veracity remained a thing to be questioned but not censured. Of course he was a poet—indeed the patriarch of the clan; and he used poetical license in his strictures on all whom publication had stamped with a small immortality.

Alison was in no danger of rivalling him in his own peculiar line—the English pentameter—so he admitted her to a share of his regard; and showed his appreciation of her culture by reciting his own verses to her, and recounting his marvellous experiences. On these occasions, standing in his broad-brimmed hat, Alec was a striking personification of the letter I. Alison frequently went in to have a chat with him; and many a weird story, many an eerie legend, or ghostly ballad did she hear in the shadow of the grey old Abbey, until the place was spectral and haunted to her imagination.

To-day Alec was nowhere visible, and she sauntered along between the rows of ruined pillars, and past St Catherine's altar, imagining the old state and grandeur of the Abbey, when its Gothic pillars and arches echoed to the tramp of vestured priests, or sounded with the chanting of stoled monks. As she pictured all this, the light around her became vari-coloured and dim; the broken columns rose up in their massive strength, and met above in the groined arches that bent over a crowd of kneeling worshippers. Rare incense floated around her, and the light of a thousand perfumed lamps threw a mystic glare upon the glittering vessels and jewelled crosses that flashed from the distant altars. The steady beat of feet rang in the dim cloisters; and nearer and nearer swelled the roll of the Latin hymn, chanted as the priestly procession passed to the high altar of St Thomas.

Alison paused bewildered.

So real was the vision, so close were the voices to her, that she could scarcely believe it was imagination that had summoned these spirits of the past before her. She glanced round confusedly. The ruined walls were still standing in their pathetic incompleteness; a withered leaf fluttered down from a tree—Time's eloquent message; the coloured light from the stained windows had faded again to wintry sunlight. Instead of the chanted liturgy she heard the hoarse clamour of the jackdaws, and the Latin hymn took the meaning of the epitaph that met her eyes from the ruined walls :—

> 'Here ly's the mortal part of Rachel Lumsden,
> Spouse was to John Niven.'

She turned from the tablet and met another inscription :—

> 'To the memory of his mother.'

'And this is the end of all the pomp and splendour,' she thought, sadly: 'a desolate shrine, a departed glory, and the record of two women's commonplace lives !'

Her ruminations were interrupted by a voice—

'Are you dreamin', Alison ?'

'I think so,' said Alison, turning with a smile to Andrew Rayne.

'I saw you come in,' he explained; 'and I wanted to ask after Jeanie. Is your hand keeping better?'

'Yes; but I must not stay to talk, Andrew, for I have to be at the Abbey House at three o'clock.'

'Then I'll wait for you here, and I want to show you a bit of a poem I've been writin'.'

Seeing that Andrew was not to be put off, Alison said no more, but hurried through the pend and into the garden that divided the house from the Abbey.

As the hour chimed from the old church, she climbed the stone staircase and rang the bell at the door of Mrs. Urquhart's residence. The door was opened by Marget, whose face reminded Alison whimsically of a cheese, for the milk of human kindness had not only soured, but grown dry and crusted with time. Her voice, too, was dry and hard and sour as she announced—

'A leddy to see you, mem.'

Alison crossed the room to the couch as Mrs. Urquhart held out her hand with a smile.

'I am not able to rise, you see. I have the pleasure of speaking to Miss——'

'I am Alison Dean,' the girl said simply. Mrs. Urquhart was too well bred to betray her astonishment, but inwardly she felt very cross with Dr. Murdoch for the manner in which he had taken her in.

He had described Alison Dean as a mill-girl, and here she was a woman of remarkable beauty, whose air, voice, and dress bespoke her refinement. It was too bad of the doctor to have played such a trick upon her! However, Mrs. Urquhart disguised her vexation, and when Alison was seated she began.

'I have been wishing for some days to see you. Was it you that injured your arm a while ago?'

'Yes,' Alison answered.

'How did you meet with the accident?'

'My arm was broken in a frame at the Ward Mill.'

Mrs. Urquhart looked puzzled. Was it true, then, that this girl was a factory worker?

'I don't understand. Do you work there?'

'Surely!' Alison exclaimed, astonished in turn.

'You must excuse me,' said Mrs. Urquhart, impulsively laying her hand on Alison's; 'but I want to know more about you. Tell me something of your parents and of yourself.'

The real kindness in voice and touch won Alison's heart; and new as it was to her to talk to a stranger, she found herself telling Mrs. Urquhart all about her life with her delicate lady-mother, and the two girls Jeanie and Liz. Then she spoke of her father, the sternly upright man, whose stainless character was her most precious possession. Mrs. Urquhart watched her enthusiasm, her proud eyes, her bright, earnest manner, and she was touched she hardly knew why.

'You are a hero-worshipper, I can see. I must try and direct your worship into other channels.'

Alison shook her head.

'That is impossible. I shall have no hero but my father.'

'Oh, not impossible at all! I fancy you will find another hero before very long. But now I want you to sing for me, if you don't mind.'

So Alison sang, her voice filling the

room with melody and sweetness; and
Mrs. Urquhart, listening, said to herself
that the song was a description of the girl
singing—

> 'Oh, my Luve's like a red, red rose
>   That's newly sprung in June;
> Oh, my Luve's like the melody
>   That's sweetly played in tune.
> So fair art thou, my bonnie lass,
>   So deep in luve am I,
> And I will luve thee still, my dear,
>   Till a' the seas gang dry.'

The last word died away in a high clear
note, but before it was quite silent Mrs.
Urquhart was speaking in a soft, beseeching voice—

'Oh, my bairn, your voice is like my
Nellie's, who died years ago. I am a
lonely old woman; will you take her place
and come to me, and be as a daughter to
me?'

The proposal was so unexpected that
Alison did not know what reply to make.

While she hesitated, Mrs. Urquhart continued, imploringly :—

'Oh, my dear! you can't tell how lonely I am, and I am so fond of having young people about me. It would be new life to have you here; and you are an orphan, and have nothing to give up. Won't you think about coming to me?'

Her quick, excited words almost took away Alison's breath.

'I don't understand,' she gasped. 'Come here?—to live with you?'

'Yes, to be my companion. I have only Marget, and you can't tell how terrible it is to lie here day after day unable to move. But if I have you for my bairn I shall have something to live for. My dear, if you will only come you shall have masters for singing, or whatever you like; and all I shall ask you to do is to brighten my life and love me a little.'

She developed her scheme as she spoke,
and, when she paused, she felt that this
improvised arrangement only needed Alison's consent to it to be spherical in its
completeness. '

And Alison was trying to grasp the
sudden idea. To live at the Abbey House;
to escape from the life of the mill; to have
masters for music and drawing, and as
many books as she wanted—it was like a
beautiful dream! Mrs. Urquhart, Alison
knew, was rich, and able to gratify herself
in expensive luxuries; but was it possible
that she meant all that she said? Instinctively she gave her a quick, searching
glance; and as she looked she felt that the
worn face, with its keen, fiercely-shining
eyes, was one to be trusted. She glanced
round the room, dark in spite of the large
window, for it was made shadowy and dim
by coloured glass. The delicate perfume

from a pot-pourri jar scented the air. A
fire dancing in the grate threw fantastic
shadows upon the walls, and touched into
glittering expression the mirrors and
artistic bric-a-brac that gave character to
the room.

In this radiant play of flame the atmosphere was vivid with colour; and the
sound of weird, faint music throbbing
through it made it full of life. Suddenly
it seemed to Alison that the elements of
the old monastic life that had so invested
the Abbey with poetry and romance had
met in this room. The vision she had
before imagined in the Abbey was here
present to her physical sight. All the
subtle charm of the monkish ritual,—music,
colour, perfume, worship, all had met in
this room; all were present in the life Mrs.
Urquhart was offering to her. She might
use them as the monks had used them;

and what would she gain? A ruined
life; the decay of her highest aspirations;
even as the walls of the Abbey, in their
ruin, were the sole memorials of that
artistic life the monks had lived. Every
priestly record had vanished. Over the
graves of the dead monks the men of to-
day, with a pathetic and bitter irony,
struggled for supremacy at bowls. The
venerable walls echoed back no name of
monk or abbot; they had a voice only for
the simple annals of domestic life, the
names of wife and mother and children.
What did this teach but that love alone
survived the shocks of time and death?

Alison saw the choice before her—the
life of art, wealth, ease, luxury: or the life
of love, a woman's practical work among
her sisters. Jeanie's mother rose up before her with a question on her dead lips.
Was she going to desert those who had

befriended her, now when they needed her most? If she accepted Mrs. Urquhart's offer she would have to leave Jeanie and Liz to struggle alone and unaided. Alison saw all this in the flash of thought that followed Mrs. Urquhart's words, and she made her choice. It was not easy for her to refuse the kind offer, and her voice broke when at last she said:

'You are very good to me. I cannot thank you enough, but it is impossible for me to leave Jeanie and Liz.'

'Not at all! You will do more for them if you come to me. Jeanie is crippled, and you will not be able to work for months. How are you to manage?'

'Mr. Carnegie has promised to continue our wages till we can work again. But it is not money; they could ill spare me from home.'

'Nonsense, child! Not one of us is

really necessary to another. Society abhors a vacuum as much as nature, and as soon as one is taken another steps in to supply his place. So Dr. Murdoch says, at any rate. You are in your wrong place at present—a round peg in a square hole—and it is hopeless for you to try and fill it. With your voice you might command anything; and as my friend, you shall have everything that money can buy—art, literature, foreign countries, all shall be open to you if you come to me.'

A thrill passed through Alison at the words; but she could not get rid of her experience in the Abbey. It seemed to tell her that the emotional, artistic life was unreal and transitory, that nothing was permanent but duty and love. Art was not life—it vanished like the splendid Abbey, and left only ruin behind it. Service and love—in these were immortality, and they awaited her in the homely life of the mills.

Alison was one of those foolish people who of two duties will choose the less agreeable. But then she had been left to God and nature for teaching, and she could not be expected to show much worldly wisdom in the conduct of life.

'Don't tempt me!' she cried, wistfully. 'My duty lies with the girls, and I can't refuse to see it.'

'Now, my dear, don't answer me all at once. Girls are so impulsive! I was, myself, when I was young. I actually refused Mr. Urquhart when he proposed; only he knew me so well he pretended to think I had said " Yes ;" and when I saw how pleased he was I hadn't the heart to undeceive him. If you distrust woman's impulse and man's honesty, you will get through life without much difficulty. Take a week to decide, and then bring me your answer.'

She was interrupted by a voice raised in angry protestation outside the door.

'I'll tak' the lad! Fat are ye fulin' aboot wi' siccan daft-like ways? Gin ye canna bide i' the hoose in peace, ye maun juist gang awa'!'

After this tirade came a slow, drawling voice :

> 'Bitter barmaid waning fast ; . . .
> What! the flower of life is past,
> It is long before you wed!'

'Ay, is it; gin I'm to wed wi' sic a man as you!' retorted a wrathful voice.

Then followed a wild shriek from the violin, whose weird music Alison had heard before. This was succeeded by the irate voice :

'Will ye no lat me to my wark, ye daft gowk?'

'Philistines arm! prepare for battle!
Gath and Askelon unite!'

sang the provokingly quiet tones to the violin accompaniment. Then the song ceased, and the drawling voice was heard—

'Your work, Delilah?—nay! 'tis pollution, and the gods forbid it. "Dagon's aid will crown the fight!"'

'Cease your heathin haverin wi' your Philistines, and your Delilah that ye should tak' shame to yersel' to name before a honest wumman! Wull ye gang your ain gate an' lat me be?'

Again the violin shrieked as he sang—

'I will defy them! I will defy them!'

Mrs. Urquhart, listening in the parlour, turned laughing to Alison.

'That is my nephew quarrelling with Marget. They are always at daggers-

drawn. Would you mind opening the
door? I must see what is the matter.'

Alison obediently opened the door, and
she could not suppress a smile at the scene
in the passage. There stood the limp form
of the poet propped against the opposite
wall, his bow feebly passing across the
strings of the violin over which his face
was bent. Beside him, built into the wall,
was a beautiful old panel of carved oak—a
relic of the wainscotting that had once
decorated the abbot's house—and before
this was the gnarled form of old Marget
brandishing a huge paste-brush that was
sprinkling the devoted poet with its sticky
burden, he standing undaunted through it
all. The whole thing was very comical,
and Alison gave a merry little laugh that
drew attention to her. Marget ceased
her hostile advance. Dante Algernon
raised his eyes and let his bow fall at

sight of the graceful figure in the door-
way.

'James,' Mrs. Urquhart called, 'come
and tell me what all this is about.'

'Excuse me, aunt, I cannot leave my
post. I am protecting this divine relic
from the onslaughts of this Philistine.
She is bent on papering the panels, and I
am preventing the desecration at the cost
of my new coat.'

Mrs. Urquhart gave a little scream.

'My panels! Marget, you mustna
touch them. I hae told you long ago I
would not have them papered. Come
away, James, she winna touch them now.'

'A gey senseless wifie that disna ken
the Screeptures,' Marget screamed, as she
raised her pail to depart. 'The Apostle
has writ, "Cleanliness is neist to godliness,"
an' hoo wull the hoose be clean sae lang as
they Pagan deils pit oot their tongues frae

the wa'? But I'll hae them ootby before the deil himsel' enter!'

The poet, seeing that the battle was over, retired to remove the 'drops of onset' still upon him; while Alison took leave of Mrs. Urquhart.

CHAPTER VIII.

ANDREW PROPOSES.

QUITE forgetful of Andrew Rayne waiting outside, she walked on, smiling at the ridiculous scene she had witnessed; but a quick step behind her recalled her to memory, and she turned to meet him.

'I thought I should not manage to overtake you. What makes you walk so fast? Didn't you wish to see me, Alison?'

'Of course I did. But I had forgotten that you were outside,' she said, as they went under the Abbey gateway.

Andrew looked a little reproachful.

'I have been waiting on you more than an hour, lassie.'

'Yes; I am very sorry. You have a poem to show me, haven't you? What is it about?'

'Luve! There's naethin' i' the warld like to it,' he said; in his excitement lapsing into broad Scotch. 'It's the a'e beauty o' life—it's like the gowan that grows for rich an' poor—it's like the sun that shines on a'—an' like the stars, aye speerin' for the morn. I canna be silent ony langer, Alison. I maun ken gin ye lo'e me, an' wad marry me!'

For the second time that afternoon Alison was thoroughly taken by surprise. But Andrew's sudden appeal moved her more than Mrs. Urquhart's. There was a warm glow at her heart responding to his words, and a beautiful flush rose to her cheek when she looked up and met his eyes full of eager hope. These, too, were eyes she could trust—calm and stedfast and earnest, with less fire but more depth in them than there was in Mrs. Urquhart's. She knew that they were windows from which looked a true, loving spirit. While she was still a girl she had learned Andrew's worth, and had recognized the artistic temperament and poetic insight that elevated his tastes and made him one of Nature's gentlemen. They were passing the Abbey wall with its old inscription, '*Rachel Lumsden, spouse was.*' Her eyes shone as she saw the words, and she thought how wonderful it was that this truest, best life had been offered her so soon after she had refused the sensuous, artistic life.

She had to say one word only, and she would gain the highest blessedness life

could offer a woman, the love of a good
man. The lashes trembled over her eyes,
a lovely colour flooded her face, and the
words that should make her Andrew's
promised wife were on her lips, when a
woman's voice, calling shrilly, rang across
the Abbey green.

'Jeanie, Jeanie; far's the lassie?'

All at once the light faded from her
face, and, like a cold finger laid on her
lips, the memory of Jeanie returned to
her and made her dumb. She remembered
that she had said to Jeanie she had only a
sister's love to give to Andrew, but she
rebelled passionately against the unnecessary sacrifice. If Andrew cared for her,
Jeanie's love was hopeless; and what right
had she to give him pain to spare the sick
girl a passing sorrow?

'Gin' Andra' disna lo'e me I maun dee!'
Jeanie's sad voice sounded in her ears, and

Alison thought wildly of the words. In the girl's weak state it might kill her to know that her love could not be returned. After all, the highest teaching demands a high price. The world is a cheap school-mistress, and the item of manners and morals is thrown in for nothing in the curriculum. Alison had learned from other teachers, and she bought her character with pain's hardest coin. The lessons she had had forbade her to purchase joy, whatever she might suffer, at another's expense. It is not an easy thing at any time to reject an offered love; but how difficult Alison found it now, only those can know whose hearts have denied the rejection of the lips.

'Andrew,' she said, brokenly, not daring to look at him lest she should waver in her resolution, 'to-day Jeanie asked me that same question—if I loved you—and I can only give you the answer I gave to her.'

'And what was that?' he asked, hoarsely; seeing from her manner there was no hope for him.

The girl needed all her self-control to answer, quietly,

'I told her I would never give you more than a sister's love——'

A quiver passed over Rayne's face, but he drew himself up in a manly fashion; and though his eyes were dark with pain, his voice betrayed no emotion.

'I hae aye feared this, Alison; I kenned you were ower guid for me, an' since Dr. Murdoch has been comin' backwards and forwards, I hinna had muckle hope.'

A great wave of colour passed over the girl's face, and she looked up indignantly at Murdoch's name. But she silenced the bitter words on her lips. It was better that he should think she cared for the doctor since he had no trust in her faithfulness to an old friend !

Andrew looked sadly at her, in her pretty gown and hat that set her at such a distance from him. He had loved Alison of the mill; and he could not wonder that this girl should prefer a gentleman like the doctor to an ordinary workingman like himself, for she had all the manner and appearance of a lady, and as Murdoch's wife would return to her own position.

'Dinna fash yersel' aboot it, Alison,' he said, ' an' dinna min' that I hae gien you the trouble o' tellin' me. I'm gaen awa' the morn, an' when I win hame you'll maybe be freends wi' me ?'

'Surely,' Alison answered, not trusting herself to say more. She was humiliated at that suggestion of his, and it added to the bitterness of her renunciation that he should misconstrue her motive.

It had cost her very little to give that promise to Jeanie when Andrew's love for her had been a remote possibility; but now when the sacrifice was piercing her heart she struggled passionately against the necessity. Yet, not only common humanity but common gratitude forbade her to do otherwise than she had done.

Jeanie's mother had befriended her when she was friendless; and now the dead woman stood, a spectral figure, and barred the gates of life that Alison would have entered. It was she who had prevented her accepting Mrs. Urquhart's offer, and now she stood in the way of love, and for her daughter's sake turned Alison from it.

The girl hid her face in her hands and sobbed aloud, and when, some minutes later, she raised her eyes, Andrew had gone, and she was alone among the graves.

She could not go on to Well's Close just then. With hurried steps she left the Abbey, and hastened on till she gained the braeheads outside the town. Here she slackened her pace, and with bursting heart gazed at the prospect before her.

Away in the distance the Seaton woods were outlined, a purple bank against the amber sky. The lately reaped fields sloped warmly coloured in the foreground; and two or three houses set in the midst of clustering trees caught the yellow glare of the sunset. The sea slept in the mellow light, and against the horizon rose the dark tower of the Bell Rock lighthouse, its red beams not yet flashing across the waters. Not a creature was in sight; and out on the lonely brae Alison did not restrain her grief.

She was very miserable, and the yellow skies and glowing landscape were out of harmony with her mood. Even the sea was still and had no voice for her pain; and not a sea-gull sent to her heart its wild shriek from the dim spaces of the sky. Nature refused to sympathise with her sorrow.

She had reached the end of the walk, and now stood irresolute at the top of the long flight of steps leading to the level ground, from which the path again rose cliffwards. Should she go on to the cliffs, or return? While she hesitated, the tall figure of a man, accompanied by a large collie dog, appeared on the Ness, and Alison thought she recognised Dr. Murdoch. If she went on she must meet him! In sudden resolution she turned and retraced her steps. And now the clouds before her had lost their radiance, and lay in sullen masses against a dark sky. The wind pierced chilly to her; and, shivering, she quickened her pace and hurried on to gain the warmth of home.

An unusual stir was about the house when she reached Well's Close, and two women stood talking to Mrs. Macintyre, who burst into tears at sight of Alison.

'Oh, the puir, mitherless bairn!' she sobbed. 'Alison, Andra' Rayne has shot himsel' the day!'

The words arrested her steps, and with white, startled face she stood looking from one to another of the women.

Andrew shot himself? Why, it was not two hours since she had spoken to him! Andrew dead—shot himself?

As ever, love was first at the grave; and it did not occur to her that the wound might not be mortal. Oh, the horror of the thought that, in despair of her rejection of him, Andrew had taken his own life. Chilled to stone, she stood with terrified eyes listening to the women, who were only too ready to detail the tragedy to the girl.

There is a piquant flavour about gossip when we know that the person listening has a vital interest in the story. The lacerating of each other's feelings is a kind of mental vivisection dear to some natures, and the neighbours in Well's Close felt that a responsibility lay upon them to break the news with so much sensational exaggeration that the girl would lay bare her real feelings to them.

But Alison did not satisfy their curiosity. She merely stood before them white and still; and her voice was calm as she asked,

'Is it true? Are you sure it is not false?'

'Ay am I, lassie. I'm juist frae the hoose. He wis lyin' in an awfu' pool o' blood, wi' his gun sittin' o' the floor beside him. I'm wae for his mither, puir widowed body!'

'An' they say, Alison,' Mrs. Macintyre added, with searching and unflinching directness—for she took a motherly interest in the girl—' they say it's a lassie's blame for it.'

'An' like eneuch, too,' said the first speaker, 'for there isna ony maitter that the lassies dinna fash themsel's wi'; an' the warld wad gae a sicht mair easy gin there wisna ony o' them in't!' Which, no doubt, is true enough.

A sympathetic sigh circulated after this reflection, but Alison wrung her hands wildly.

'Oh, I don't believe it! He can't have done it himself!'

'An' wha else wad dae a deed like that? Ye wadna be thinkin' it was murder, surely!' Mrs. Macintyre said reproachfully.

'Murder? Ay is it!' said a voice behind them.

The women turned round sharply and stared at the new comer, Bell Macniel, who came forward full of importance with the latest intelligence.

'It's murder, clear eneuch,' she said. 'Dr. Lindsay came in bye, an' as sune as he had a sicht o' Andra' he said the lad couldna hae shot himsel', for the bullet wis in his neck. The police are awa' to the hoose, an' M'Nab says somebody 'll swing for it!'

Alison did not stop to hear more. She turned away with an instinctive desire to hide her grief from the curious eyes fixed upon her. But she forgot herself when she reached the attic and met Liz, who, with frightened face, was at the door.

'Oh, Alison!' she screamed, 'Jeanie's awa'. I heard her gie a scream-like as I came up the stair, an' I cried to her that I wis comin', an' when I cam' in by I got her this way.'

Alison pushed past Liz and rushed to the bedside.

'Go for the doctor, Liz!' she cried. 'Don't lose a minute, go as fast as you can!'

'I kenned weel she was deid,' Liz sobbed, not daring to look at Jeanie's still form. 'Like eneuch they hae tellt her aboot Andra'. Hae ye heard fat's cam' to him?'

'Yes, yes,' Alison cried wildly. 'But don't stop. Run, Liz; get the doctor, he may save her yet!'

'Is she no deid?' said Liz, with her hand on the latch.

'I don't know! I can't tell! Why do you stand talking? Go right away at once!' Alison cried, stamping her foot impatiently as Liz still lingered.

The girl was scarcely conscious, but Alison's sharp voice roused her, and she ran down the steps and into the close without stopping to speak to the women, who called to ask what was to do with Jeanie.

CHAPTER IX.

THROUGH THE LONG NIGHT.

Liz met Dr. Murdoch before she had gone very far. She stopped, out of breath, as the doctor accosted her.

'I'm just away to Jeanie. Has she heard this about Rayne?'

'Ay,' Liz said, with a sob. 'She's heard, an' she's awa'. Alison bade me say would you come to her.'

'Na, na, lassie; she's no awa' yet. Come wi' me the noo, and you'll soon see she's no deid.'

Murdoch spoke cheerfully, but he knit

his brows anxiously. In Jeanie's weak condition the shock might have been fatal. It
was to prevent her hearing the news
suddenly that he had hurried away to
Well's Close; but he had been too late,
and the girl already knew of Andrew's
peril.

He quickened his steps. Liz could not
keep up with his rapid strides; so he went on
in front, leaving her to follow more slowly.
For all his anxiety, it was not at Jeanie
that he glanced first as he entered the
room, but at Alison; and before she could
speak he poured out a glass of wine from
a bottle on the table, and bade her drink
it.

Alison took the glass from him, her
great eyes so full of agony that he could
not meet her look. With love's intuition
he knew that all her dumb pain was not
for Jeanie. He touched her arm gently,

and said—but his voice was so strange and hoarse that she scarcely heard the words :—

'You must not be over-anxious, he may recover !'

Alison set down the glass, and gazed wildly at him.

'Recover!   Oh, Dr. Murdoch!   Isn't he dead ?'

He gave her a shy, scared look, and then drew himself up, and with an assumption of indifference, answered carelessly,

'Dead! not he!   They thought so at first, but life is not extinct, and——'

Alison gave a great sob, and before Murdoch could complete his sentence, she caught his hand and kissed it suddenly. A flush rose to his face, and the silence that followed the act might have been embarrassing had he not summoned to his aid all his professional coolness.

'No, he is not dead,' he said, quietly; 'and what's more, Miss Alison, if *I* can save him he'll not die. You know they say it's murder, but I'm not so sure of that. It's certain he didn't shoot himself, but it may have been an accident. However, no one can tell that till Rayne is able to speak. I hope to goodness he'll do that before he dies, else it may be awkward for somebody.'

He glanced sharply at the girl, but she did not seem to be listening to him. Her whole air was elevated, her eyes shining, her face radiant. She looked as Mary might have looked when she received Lazarus from the grave. While his hand still tingled from the sudden contact with her lips, his brow clouded and he felt a pang of jealous pain. Then he became savage with himself that he had forgotten that Alison's gratitude was called forth for the life of her *lover !*

'I must see to my patient,' he said, coldly, advancing to the bed.

At this moment Liz entered the room.

'Oh, Alison, I ken by your face that Jeanie's no deid!'

The doctor had a keen sense of humour, and he was a young man. In spite of his jealous rage, as Liz spoke, for the life of him he could not help looking mischievously at Alison. The cynical smile on his face flooded Alison's cheek with the deepest confusion, and she blushed so painfully that he repented him of his malice and averted his gaze instantly.

Jeanie was to all appearance dead; but he saw in a moment that she had only swooned, and he bent his energies towards restoring her to consciousness. It was long before

M 2

his efforts were successful, but at length she gave a long, shuddering sigh and opened her eyes.

'Andra'!—Oh, Alison! He's deid by his ain hand!'

Her eyelids trembled again over her eyes, and she seemed to be sinking once more into that deathly stupor; but Murdoch rose and lifted her hand from the coverlet.

'What's wrang wi' you, Jeanie?' he said. 'The lad's richt eneuch;—wha tellt you he'd killed himsel'? Na, na, lassie, it's no true. His brains are ower guid for him to throw them awa' without rhyme or reason, especially without rhyme!'

His words roused the girl. She opened her eyes again and looked at him.

'That's right!' he said. 'Look at me, and I'll tell you the whole truth. The lad's been shot, like enough, by accident; but he'll no die, if I can prevent it!'

Jeanie drank in the words with a hungry light in her eyes that revealed the secret of her love for Andrew to the three watching her. She was effectually roused, but Murdoch saw that she would scarcely rally from the shock she had had, and he went away, promising to look in again that night.

Going home he mused on the scene he had witnessed. Of course he knew nothing about love,—so he said with a shrug of his shoulders,—but he would be very much mistaken if each one of the three girls he had left did not love Andrew Rayne.

Poor Jeanie had betrayed herself; and he had observed the terror in Liz's face, and seen it was not all called forth by her sister's danger. As for Alison—the kiss was proof positive that she cared for Andrew. The doctor, with a strange thrill, felt his hand burning; and he drew off his glove and looked curiously at his long psychical hand. There was a great deal of character in it, and one might safely predict that in the operating room it would be cold and calm and skilful; apt in the use of shining steel. It was gentle and tender as a woman's in the sick-room—but it could be cruel and murderous in its strength! And it was this white, cruel-looking hand that Alison had kissed, he thought to himself. He must have had a feeling of guilt, for after this thought he glanced round quickly to see if he had been observed—and there was May Lindsay hurrying to overtake him!

Then Murdoch did a curious thing, for he deliberately drew on his glove before he offered his hand to May!

It was late when he returned to Well's Close. He found Jeanie in a heavy, trancelike sleep ; Alison sitting pale and anxious beside her. Liz was asleep on two chairs near the fire, looking very pretty, with her flushed face and bright hair falling over the dark red gown she wore. The doctor would not disturb her, and after he had looked at Jeanie he beckoned Alison to follow him into the room across the landing.

'I don't wish to alarm you,' he said kindly ; ' but she has had a severe shock. You should be prepared for the worst.'

Alison looked up startled.

' The worst ! Oh, Dr. Murdoch ! And Andrew dying too !' She clutched at the table by which she stood, and as Murdoch saw her emotion a dark look passed across his face. He placed a chair for her, saying quickly,

' You must not give way, now. Rayne may not die. I have just come from him.

I think he will pull through; I am sure
I hope so, for Alec's sake. The town is in
arms against him, saying he shot Rayne.
It's all a pack of nonsense!'

Alison looked up at the impatient tones.

'Alec? Why, he and Andrew were
great friends!'

'Oh, yes; but Alec's fond of money,
and he was seen counting out some to
Andrew in the cottage. No one saw him
leave the place, and half-an-hour after
Rayne was found shot. The curious
thing is, that no money has been found
in the house, and Alec had a bag with
twenty sovereigns on him when he was
searched.'

Alison's face quivered.

'How wicked people are! They will
think any evil of their friends. But,
about Jeanie——'

'Ah, yes! I'm afraid there's not much

hope for her; she may not get through the night, or she may linger for days. You have had a great deal to bear?'

'Yes,' Alison whispered; and then she laid her head on the table and sobbed in her bitter grief.

The doctor took two or three turns up and down the room before he paused and looked down at the bowed head, with its great masses of hair all tossed and tumbled. He had admired her in her strength and self-control, but something deeper than admiration was stirred now, as he saw her in her girlish weakness and sorrow. How like a child she looked in her abandonment! How like a child! And yet had ever child so hard a lot?— to stand between two death-beds and face the parting from the two she loved most on earth—her lover and her almost sister? Murdoch was used to scenes like this.

He had to witness daily the deepest
sorrows of life and death, but Alison's
grief appealed to him personally, and his
heart ached for her. A great pity and
longing stirred in his heart. He would
have given anything to have had the right
to take her in his arms and comfort her,
and let her know that she was not utterly
desolate. But between him and Alison
stood the figure of Andrew Rayne, and
the dying man seemed to lift a finger
forbidding him to touch the girl he loved.
Restraining himself with a great effort,
he spoke quietly—

'You must be strong, for Jeanie's sake,'
he said, striking the chord he knew would
soonest vibrate to his touch. 'She has
no one but you; and you will be glad she
should be spared further suffering. It's
a better business that she should go now
quietly and painlessly, for if she had lived

she must have lost her leg; and I fear she could not have survived the operation.'

Alison's sobs broke out afresh.

'Poor little child! Poor little Alison!' he said, half-aloud, not knowing how to comfort her.

She looked up at the words, her eyes streaming with tears, and she put her hand in his. The doctor was strongly moved, and his eyes were full of the light of love as he clasped her hand close, and bent towards her uplifted face, looking wildly into her swimming eyes. His breath was on her cheek, and he felt her hand tightening in his—

'And Andrew?' she said. 'Must he, too?'

He started as though he had been stung, and let her hand fall, while he turned savagely from her beseeching glance. Was the figure of Rayne always to come between himself and Alison?

He resumed the professional manner he had laid aside during the last few minutes.

'I can tell you no more about him. But you must not sit up alone to-night. I'll go and send Mrs. Macintyre to you. I'll not leave you myself till there's a change.'

Alison had no need to ask why it was necessary for him to remain. She understood too well.

'Mrs. Macintyre is away to-night. I'll go in and waken Liz.'

'No, don't do that; she will hinder more than help you. I'll sit here by the fire, and you can call me if I'm needed.'

He opened the door for Alison, and she went through to the next room, leaving the doctor to his thoughts. For a time everything was quiet, but after a while he thought he heard voices in the next room. Through the open door across the landing he could see that the lamp had burned low, but the firelight brightened the room and showed Liz still asleep. Alison was bending over Jeanie, and one glance showed him that she lay in 'the sleep that knows no waking.'

While he looked his heart beat quickly at the pitiful cry that rang through the room—

'Jeanie! Jeanie! I have lost every-thing!'

He could not restrain himself, and in a strange, husky voice he called aloud,

'Alison! my darling, come to me. I love you; I will care for you always!'

Would she come to him? In intense excitement he waited for her next move-ment. She rose slowly and turned her face towards him, and it was shining with a rare beauty. He watched her come forward, and as he gazed everything in the room faded. The lamp went out, and he could not see Liz asleep, or Jeanie's still form on the bed. He saw nothing but the radiance on Alison's face as she came to him through the flashing firelight and laid her hand in his—

'Dr. Murdoch, I have come——'

He started violently. Yes, it was quite true; he was alone with Alison, her hand was on his, and the flames showed that she was standing before him, while he heard, clearly enough—

'Dr. Murdoch, I have come for you. I think there is a change.'

Still half-asleep, he rose and followed her to the bedside. He was dazed and confused, but he knew he had been sleeping, and all that he had seen had been a dream only. Jeanie was not dead, but she was gasping for breath, and he seated himself on the bed and supported her head on his shoulder, while Alison moistened her lips with wine. Then she too sat down; and in silence, and almost in darkness, they began their long watch by the side of the dying girl.

Association in deep sorrow brings us nearer to each other's heart than association in joy; and, sitting there in the presence of death, Alison and the doctor were drawn nearer to each other than they would have been by months of ordinary intercourse. They came so near that the shadows even now deepening over Murdoch's head hung close above them both. But the light that caused the shadow was already shining in the girl's heart; and on that night was lighted the love and trust that would make his grief hers when the black cloud of guilt should hang darkly above him.

And so the long night wore through, and when the pale dawn entered the room that had so nearly seen a paler presence, Jeanie slept softly on the doctor's arm.

The robin in the lilac bush outside looked out from his feathers with a feeble chirp, and roused the sparrows, who began to twitter as they gazed sleepily at the waking world. All the subtle stir of morning was in the air, and Murdoch looked across at Alison.

'I should go now. She is asleep, but if you will help me I can put her down without waking her.'

As they laid Jeanie back on the pillow their hands touched, and then Murdoch knew that he loved Alison as a man in his life loves but one woman.

He knew also that the figure of Andrew Rayne stood between himself and his love!

Two hours after in came Mrs. Lindsay. In her sharp, bird-like manner, she stepped on tiptoe to the bed, her head on one side like an attentive canary's. Alison rose to meet her.

'I know, I know,' chirped the little woman, not giving the girl time to speak. 'Dr. Murdoch has told me everything. He makes a point of confessing his sins to me; knows I would hear them from other people if he didn't! I've sent him off to bed. He insisted on seeing that poor young lad Rayne before he had had his breakfast, and I met him with a face so white that it would have been the death of any patient that saw it suddenly. He's not been in bed for a week, so I am just taking his work for him this morning. And how do you feel, Jeanie?'

'I'm fine the day, mem, but I'm no carin' to live, wi' Andra' deein'. Gin Liz wis merried an' settled I should be happy to dee the noo.'

'Look here, child,' said Mrs. Lindsay, sharply, 'be quite easy about Liz. I promise to see after her. If ever she wants a friend I'll take charge of her. Is there anything you would like?'

'I wad like weel to ken gin Andra' is ony waur the morn.'

'Worse? Not he! Dr. Murdoch's got a fine new drug that is to cure him, so you must just make haste and get better yourself.'

'Na, na. I ken weel I'll sune be awa'. But I'm no feart. Alison says I canna get beyont God's love. But, eh! it's dark-like. Wull I win hame, dae you think?'

'Yes, my poor lammie; you needna fear. It's all dark-like, and we know nothing,

but where there's love there'll be home
for us all!'

Mrs. Lindsay's jerky tones were low
and tender, and her cold, grey eyes were
suspiciously dim.

Jeanie felt the loving heart under the
sharp exterior, and she laid her hand
gratefully on Mrs. Lindsay's.

'You're very kind,' she said.

'Toots! toots! Now I'll run away—I
have fifteen patients to see before dinner.
Dr. Murdoch is so unreasonable; if he
get's a patient ill he's no satisfied to let
Nature cure him. He'll be in to see you
later, Jeanie. Alison, you are looking
very pale; you must take care of yourself.'

With a quick, little nod she tiptoed to
the door, and they heard her high heels,
the only feminine weakness Mrs. Lindsay
allowed herself, tap-tapping all the way

down the stairs. She had scarcely gone
when there was another knock at the door,
and the grim face of Mrs. Urquhart's
Marget looked in. She handed a note to
Alison as she entered.

'This letter is for you, I'm thinkin'.
An' is't true that yon lassie's deein'? Eh
deary, deary! but she looks awfu' like it!'

She stood looking pitifully at Jeanie for
a while.

'The prophet says that God tempers
the win' to the clippit yow, but I'm dootin'
He's no been mindin' o' this ane, puir
lammie! Weel, lassie, gin ye're ane o'
His ain He winna be a'thegither unmindfu'
o' you. Ye'll no be lang i' this weary
warld, sae I'll juist speer gin ye're ane o'
the elect?'

'She is not equal to much talking,'
Alison said. 'You see she is very weak.'

'Weak? Ay, is she! Onybody wi' ae

e'e i' her heid could see that the cratur's weak, but I wis speerin' gin she wis wicket as weel as weak. My wean,' she continued, leaning over the bed, ' I wad ken gin ye're ane o' the elect; ane o' the Lord's ain bairns?'

'I dinna ken,' said Jeanie, wearily: 'I'm i' the dark whiles, but I ken that I love Him.'

Marget looked up with horror in her face.

'She disna ken gin she's o' the elect! She's i' the verra thraw o' death, an' she disna ken! Bairn, bairn, you maun bide till I get oor meenister to you. He'll snatch ye fra your doots like a brand fra the burnin'. Mony hae I seen tremblin' i' his jedgements: mony o' the sainted deid has he frichtened richt into Paradise at the last hoor, like Lazarus i' Abram's boosom, the Lord be thankit! I'll juist rin an' lead him to you, ere it be too late!'

A shadow of trouble passed over Jeanie's face.

'Alison,' she cried, 'is't true? Am I no richt for Heaven? A kirk member, Alison, an' I hae aye loved Him?'

'That winna stan' gin ye're no ane o' the elect,' Marget began sternly. 'I'm dootin' you're a wean o' the deil's ain, but I'll send Mr. Macculloch in to you. Guid day to ye baith.'

That evening Jeanie had many visitors.

All her companions at the mill, learning that she had not long to live, came in to take farewell of her. Jeanie's life at the mill was over, but she would still live there in her friends' memories; and for many years the girls would tell the story of the gentle worker whose death had been as brave and calm as her life had been pure and true.

Through the night Liz and Alison watched beside her, and when it was dawn the end came.

She had not stirred for some hours, but when the bell rang out for six o'clock she woke.

'Alison!' she cried, in a clear, high voice—'There's the bell. The gates wull sune be open. Wull I gae in the day?'

'Yes, Jeanie,' Alison answered through her tears, for she knew well Jeanie was very near entering through the gates into the city.

'I can hear them comin' in, Alison—like the soun' o' mony watters—a great multitude singin'. I'd like fine to hear you singin' wi' them, Alison; ane o' your ain auld sangs.'

So, with breaking voice, Alison sang, while Jeanie's face became bright with a wonderful light of gladness—

'So I'm watchin' aye, an' singin' o' my hame as I wait
  For the soun'in' o' His fitfa' this side the gowden gate ;
  God gie His grace to ilka ane wha listens noo to me,
  That a' may gang in gladness to oor ain countrie.'

But neither of the two watching her was able to tell when in Jeanie's ear the sound of Alison's song mingled with the voice of the great multitude singing.

CHAPTER X.

AT THE ABBEY HOUSE.

'DR. MURDOCH,' said Mrs. Urquhart, laughingly, 'it is actually a week since you have been in to see me, and a serious complication has arisen meanwhile.'

'Yes?' said the doctor, looking quizzically at her; for since Alison had gone to live at the Abbey House Mrs. Urquhart's health and spirits had wonderfully improved. 'Yes? Has Mrs. Lindsay been attending you?'

'You need not insinuate anything against Mrs. Lindsay, doctor; she is an admirable woman, the very wife for a medical man. You should marry a Lindsay, Dr. Murdoch!'

The doctor's face was a little confused, but he carried it bravely.

'By Jove!' he exclaimed. 'She *is* an admirable woman! She saw fifteen of my patients, and cured seven of them in one visit. That results from women entering the profession—they are so emotional that in their zeal they forget the common conditions of existence. Starve the doctor and cure the patient is their motto. Fancy effecting a cure in one visit! What man in his senses ever did it?'

Mrs. Urquhart shook her finger at him.

'It's no use; you will not take me from the subject. Do you know you are making poor May Lindsay very jealous?'

The doctor's complexion became a bright terra-cotta.

' I don't understand—I ? Jealous ? What
do you mean ?'

He looked very young and ingenuous in
his confusion, and Mrs. Urquhart thought
what a very nice fellow he was; but,
woman-like, she would not spare him!

' Yes,' she said, severely, ' you are making May jealous. Yesterday Alison was
at the mill, and May came here to her tea
with old Miss Mansel. You have been
attending her lately, haven't you?'

' Yes; a case of dyspepsia, aggravated
by imagination. She is one of Mrs. Lindsay's trophies; cured at a sitting !'

' Well, she was telling us of your kind —
indeed, *very* kind attentions; and she was
so conscious and girlish that May's sus-
picions were aroused. And when Miss
Mansel went on to tell how you sat holding her hand all through the last visit,

May saw that there was no hope for her.'

' It's a lee !' roared the doctor, with one of his heartiest laughs—' the auld sinner ! It's a lee !'

He looked immensely relieved, and Mrs. Urquhart smiled at the success of her strategy.

'Very well then, it's not Miss Mansel. But I'm no sure it's not some one else, for you looked very guilty just now. Seriously, doctor, you know you have only to ask for May Lindsay ! She would make you a good wife. She hasn't her mother's common sense, but she has all her father's shrewdness and worldly wisdom.'

' Well, the truth is, Dr. Lindsay has given me a hint on the subject, and at one time I might have thought about it. He offered to make over the practice to me, you know. But it won't do. May is very pretty, but a man needs something more in a wife than a pretty companion. What do you think?'

'Well, I don't know. Those ideas are rather old-fashioned. Girls—at least the plain ones—used to think so when I was young; but things are altered now. All the men run after a pretty face, without considering if there is anything behind it.'

'If there is anything, it's usually a bad temper!' the doctor said. 'No, no, Mrs. Urquhart, I'm not to marry for beauty.'

'So my little friend May is not to be Mrs. Murdoch? You are ill to please, doctor!'

'I don't think so,' he said, boyishly; and Mrs. Urquhart was amused to see an unwonted shyness on his frank face.

'I know what my ideal woman is like, for I met her once. Brave and unselfish, self-controlled and gentle; and—yes, she was beautiful, too; but you never thought of her beauty, it was her goodness that struck you most.

'Her eyes are homes of silent prayer——'

He broke off suddenly, and abstractedly gazed into the fire.

'Then, doctor, you did not deserve to meet her if you could not go farther. What hindered?'

'She cared for some one else,' he said; and his thoughts wandered from Mrs. Urquhart's pretty room to a bare attic where a dark head was bowed on a table, and a girl was weeping for her lover's peril.

Mrs. Urquhart looked disappointed and foiled; for lately there had come into her life a new zest—the desire to make a match between her favourite doctor and her almost daughter Alison.

'And may I know who she was?' she asked, quietly.

Dr. Murdoch looked up with the sharp decision of a resolute man.

'Yes, I should like to tell you. Her name is——'

The door opened. There was a stir of voices and laughter, and three gay faces invaded the *tête-à-tête*. Alison came in first, her eyes dancing, her cheeks aflame with healthy colour. No longer the quiet Alison of Well's Close, but a happy girl glad in the consciousness of a guarded womanhood. She crossed the room with light, free step and shook hands with the doctor, turning with a tender inquiry to Mrs. Urquhart. Only the doctor took note of this; May and the poet were too full of some merry jest to care about any one else. May's laughter ceased when she caught sight of the doctor, and there was a proud little air of disdain about her as she gave him her hand. It seemed to her that Dr. Murdoch spent most of his time at the Abbey House now!

The poet's gaiety also suddenly subsided, and gave place to a languid acquiescence in fate's arrangements.

'How do?' he said, extending two limp fingers to the doctor.

'How do?' said Murdoch, meeting this munificent offer with two rigid digital extremities.

The cordiality of the hand-shake resulting did not disturb the poet's equanimity. He threw himself on the couch and fell to worshipping a blue-china plate on the opposite wall.

'Mrs. Urquhart,' May cried gaily, regaining her spirits, 'we have had such fun. We went on the cliffs, and we met old Mr. Macculloch sauntering along—you know his abstracted way?—carrying a dead rat! Mr. Robinson thought he saw a Peter-Bell-and-the-primrose sort of meaning in the act—the germ of a sonnet, he said, and he insisted on stopping to talk to Mr. Macculloch. You can't imagine how absurd he was.'

'Mr. Macculloch!' interpolated the poet.

'Yes, Mr. Macculloch!' May agreed. 'What do you think he told us? He said he had left his sermon in the pulpit last Sunday, and he went to-day to look for it. He couldn't discover the manuscript anywhere, but in the vestry he found this dead rat, and actually there was a bit of the sermon sticking in its throat. So he took it up, and brought it out to the cliffs to help his meditations.'

'I took the fellow in my hand,' said the poet, mildly. 'He was stiff and very heavy. I fancy he had eaten all the sermon!'

Dr. Murdoch roared outright.

'Many a sermon sticks in my throat, I can tell you. I don't wonder Mr. Macculloch's killed the rat. Well, did you discover the germinal sonnet?'

The poet shook his head sadly.

'In all death, even that of a rat, there is poetry and a tragic beauty; but the minister's presence spoiled it.'

'James, I'm ashamed of you!' said Mrs. Urquhart vigorously. 'There is more tragic beauty in Mr. Macculloch's lonely and unselfish life than in fifty dead rats. I can tell you it is not only rats who lose all life and vitality in trying to subsist on manuscripts.'

This palpable hit delighted the doctor, and he roared again at the lady's wit.

'You are severe, aunt,' murmured the poet, 'and I have already suffered to-day from the vigour of Miss Alison and her criticisms.'

'Yes,' May cried merrily; 'Alison wrote a parody on one of the " Heart Throes," and we were laughing at it when we came in. Do read it again, Alison. It is called " *The Ballade of the Ruminant Rye.*" '

'But what does that mean?' Mrs. Urquhart asked. 'You must tell me before you begin.'

'It means nothing,' May said. 'It is like one of the " Heart Throes." But you will see when Alison reads. Do begin, Alison.'

So Alison began obediently:

> 'Beneath the spell of Nature's wand
>   He loved ere yet he wist;
> He shook Bianca's little hand;
>   Tobias shook his fist !
>
> As swift before the welkin storm
>   He watched the white mists roll,
> He blessed Bianca's massive form;
>   Tobias blessed his soul !

One eve through all the moonlit land
  He walked with languid pride ;
Bianca held his pliant hand,
  Tobias held his side.

" Our souls are one, my own, my own !
  One through all life—through death !"
Bianca caught the dulcet tone,
  Tobias caught his breath !

The dew was falling, it was chill,
  Nay damp, that summer eve ;
He took Bianca up the hill ;
  Tobias took his leave !'

The poet listened dreamily. After all,
it was something to know that one beside
himself had peered into the mysteries of
' Heart-Throes,' even though it had only
been to parody the musical murmurs of
the ' *Legende of the Languorous Lux !*'
Alison read the verses with a dainty enjoyment of their absurdity that was very
charming, though they roused bitter
thoughts in Murdoch's mind :—for was he
not in the case of Tobias, standing by to
see Bianca carried off by the nameless, but
too-successful ' He ' ?

While she read he had an excuse for fixing his eyes upon her; and, like most people who come into possession of a good excuse, he made the most of it. He took note of every detail of the change that had come over her since that night, three months ago, when they had watched together by Jeanie's death-bed. It was the same Alison, the same pleasant face with the kind eyes looking frankly from it; but this girl before him bore the same resemblance to the Alison he had first known that the rose-bush in July bears to the rose-bush in December. This was Alison in blossom; this girl with saucy lips and flashing eyes, gracefully poised head, and air of radiant beauty.

Alison in blossom! But his hands might never gather the flower for himself. Before this tree of life stood the angel of death, and above the flashing sword it

held shone the warning eyes of Andrew
Rayne!

When Alison finished reading she looked
up brightly and unexpectedly;—so quickly
that the doctor, watching her, was taken
off his guard, and allowed her to see a
look on his face she had never met there
before. A curious thrill passed through
her, and she coloured under the eyes fixed
on her with such meaning. Her confusion
was so perceptible that Murdoch rose
hurriedly and walked to the window.

'How bright the weather is for this time
of the year,' he said, snatching at the
straw which has saved many a conversation from drowning in the seas of silence.
'It hardly seems like December, does it?'

No one replied immediately to this
startlingly-novel observation.

May was full of jealous anger, for she
had seen the look that had upset Alison's

composure. The poet's thoughts were engaged with Tobias and Bianca; and Mrs. Urquhart was saying to herself how tiresome it was that her *tête-à-tête* with the doctor should have been interrupted at its most interesting point. She had not suspected that he had had a love-story already. Who could that beautiful woman have been? After all, it was Alison that came to the doctor's assistance in rescuing the conversation from drowning.

'It has been quite warm and sunny to-day; May and I are thinking of going to the Redhead to-morrow.'

'You will enjoy that,' he said quickly. 'I should like to go myself, but I have to see a patient in the country.'

'Will you allow me to go?' the poet asked softly.

'I am afraid the walk would be too much for you,' Alison said, with pretty irony. 'We are going along the cliffs as far as Auchmithie, then inland through Ethie woods to the Redhead, then home by the cliffs again.'

'Miss Alison, spare me, I beg!' exclaimed the poet with horror. 'The bare recital of your energy unnerves me. Dear ladies, is there any poetry, any rhythm, in those pedestrian exercises?'

'I think so,' Alison said saucily. 'There are feet in rhythm and poetry? why should there not be poetry and rhythm in feet?'

He turned upon her a look of gentle reproach. Surely Nature erred in putting a healthy soul into so beautiful a garb! He had been tempted to walk to the Redhead, but a whole day with the robust and healthy physique of this fair barbarian before him was too great a price to pay for the pleasure.

Sitting at supper with her that night, after the doctor and May had gone home together, he could not help wishing that she had been a woman of the higher cult. She was so dainty and charming that it was a thousand pities that Nature had not added the crowning charm of delicate inanity; the charm that would have gained her a place among the fair ones enshrined in 'Heart-Throes.' But Alison refused to fit herself for the immortality that lay between the white and gold covers of that inspired volume. She was wholesomely natural, and her young appetite made him shudder! Yet he would not confess to himself how much her residence at the Abbey House had had to do with his continued stay at Arbroath.

By-and-by Alison threw a bright glance at him.

'Do you know that this house is

haunted, Mr. Robinson? Last night Alec saw a white figure cross the green at midnight and pass into the cellars. Suppose we sit up for it to-night?'

'Don't be rash,' Mrs. Urquhart said. 'It is never well to tempt Providence.'

The lady evidently had the poor opinion of the ability of Providence to resist temptation that is common to most people.

' And,' she continued, 'don't let Marget hear you scoffing, for she has a great respect for bogles. She has seen my wraith more than once, and on each occasion she warned me that my doom was near.'

'That is thoughtful of her,' said the poet; 'calculated to be so reassuring. By the way, aunt, isn't the bowling-green laid over the graves of the old monks?'

'Yes; and on Hallowe'en they rise and have a game. I believe they use their own skulls for bowls, but you must take Alec's word for that.'

Alison laughed.

'In that case it would be worth while sitting up to see how it is managed.'

Dante Algernon shuddered.

'Miss Alison, it is not well to be frivolous; one never knows how near to us the ghosts may be.'

'Alec is no like to be frivolous just now,' Mrs. Urquhart said. 'Marget is in great trouble because he is still under suspicion of shooting and robbing young Rayne. I suppose he'll be kept under supervision till Rayne is able to give evidence against him.'

'Dr. Murdoch says he thinks Andrew was shot by accident,' Alison said quietly.

'Oh, likely enough. But, if it hadna been for Dr. Murdoch's skill in saving Rayne, I'm thinking Alec would have been on his trial for murder before this.'

'Why in the world doesn't Rayne speak and clear up the mystery?' said the poet, impatiently.

'Dr. Murdoch will not allow him to be questioned till his recovery is certain,' Alison answered.

'Have you been to see him to-day, my bairn?' Mrs. Urquhart asked.

'I called at the house,' Alison said, colouring, 'but his mother would not let me go in.'

CHAPTER XI.

ANDREW RAYNE.

MAY was at the Abbey House early next morning, and found Alison ready for the expedition to the Redhead. She had been easily persuaded to accept Mrs. Urquhart's offer after Jeanie's death, for Mrs. Lindsay had taken Liz to live with her, and her responsibility for the Munroes was over. Liz liked her new life. After the freedom of the mill, the confinement might have been irksome, but she was learning dressmaking and millinery and hair-dressing—arts she found useful in the adornment of her own pretty little person.

There was also plenty of stir in her new life; a constant excitement of doctors coming and going, that reconciled her to giving up the freedom of Well's Close.

Alison had taken charge of the Guild for the mill girls, which was now working successfully; and her time was occupied by masters who came down from Dundee to give her lessons in music and painting.

May Lindsay shared these lessons; and in working with Alison she forgot her old feud and became friends, professing a warm attachment to the girl she had despised. It is true that she admired Alison, but it was the suspicion that Dr. Murdoch shared this admiration which was at the root of this sudden friendship. She saw a future combat between them approaching; and with the worldly wisdom to which Mrs. Urquhart had alluded, she decided that Alison, as a friend, would be a less dangerous rival than Alison as an enemy.

Alison, in her simplicity, never doubted the sincerity of May's gushing attachment for her, but wondered at and was grateful to her for it. May's affection was a pretty thing, and it raised her immensely in Dr. Murdoch's estimation; for, he said, there must be something very noble in a girl who can yield such lovely homage to nobility in another—women as a rule were so jealous of each other.

Clearly there was more in May than he had thought at first; and, perhaps, if he had not met Alison Dr. Lindsay's wishes might have had some weight with him. But here the doctor checked himself. It was impossible that any woman could ever be to him what Alison had been, even though he had no hope of making her his wife. Since he had known her his friends had observed a subtle, undefined change in him. He was higher in tone, more refined in accent and manner, more gentle and chivalrous than he had been. His boyish gaiety was giving way to a manly earnestness, and he was more sympathetic than in the days when success in his profession had been a strong incentive to friendliness.

His attendance on Andrew Rayne had perhaps to do with this change. It was owing to Murdoch's untiring skill that Rayne had not succumbed to his injuries. That promise to Alison had been well kept, and the doctor had not spared himself in his efforts to save the life of his rival.

This morning, when Alison and May were about to start for their long walk, the mystery surrounding Andrew had been cleared up. Going home through the Abbey after Alison's rejection of him, he had stopped to speak to Alec, and to ask his advice about taking a situation that had been offered him as librarian of a large public library in Nottingham.

Alec's advice was always shrewd and far-seeing; and from the growing of a beard to the choice of a sweetheart there was no subject upon which he was not consulted by the young lads of Arbroath. It was, therefore, quite natural that Andrew should consult him before deciding to leave the town where he had won poetic fame (and a very scanty living) for the wider sphere of Nottingham: before descending from the hungry heights of Parnassus to the homely level of well-remunerated labour!

He was a dreamy fellow, and he would have been well content to have settled down in Arbroath writing his little poems and painting his little pictures. But love had pierced through the stratum of poetic clay to the spring of practical good sense, and had brought the clear waters to the surface. Looking into their depths, he saw clearly the life he must live if he would be worthy of Alison.

To be a successful man, and a worthy rival of Dr. Murdoch, something more was needed than publishing (unpaid) poems in the *Arbroath Argus*, or painting pictures whose value money could not—at least it did not!—measure. He must get into the world and struggle with the hard conditions of life.

London, with its vivid literary life, began to draw him, as it draws all men of intellectual activity. He began to long for books—books! To get into the whirl of the vortex where he would be carried round in the rushing life of thought. Nottingham was nearer London than Arbroath, but he had two strong reasons for refusing the post offered him through the interest of a friend. First, he had not enough money to take him to England: secondly, by quitting Arbroath he would be leaving Alison open to the attentions of the doctor, and would thus lose all chance of winning her.

Rayne's was one of those rare masculine natures that can see possibilities for the rival that contests the field with him. Alec soon had the story of his rejection, and of the offered post at Nottingham; and with uncommon generosity, for he knew the value of the bawbee, he offered to lend Andrew the sum necessary to start him in England.

The old man had a large and varied experience in love-making;—it was whispered that he had a weakness for the ladies, but this must have been a libel on

his practical wisdom and common-sense!
And now he told Andrew that his absence
from Arbroath would be the very thing to
draw Alison's thoughts to him.

'The way to win a lassie, Andra' lad, is
to treat her as gin ye hadna muckle thocht
o' her,' he said.   'Wummen are awfu'
contrairy; an' you need but flout them to
get them to mak' up to you themsel's.
You ken fat oor ain Robbie says :—

> " Duncan fleech'd, and Duncan pray'd ;
> Meg was deaf as Ailsa Craig ;
> Duncan sighed baith out an' in,
> Grat his een baith bleer't an' blin',
> Spak' o' lowpin ower a linn !
>
> Time an' chance are but a tide,
> Slighted love is sair to bide ;
> Shall I, like a fool, quoth he,
> For a haughty hizzie dee?
> She may gae to—France for me !
>
> How it comes let doctors tell ;
> Meg grew sick as he grew heal ;
> Something in her bosom wrings,
> For relief a sigh she brings ;
> An' oh, her een, they spak' sic' things !" '

Andrew smiled sadly.   Alison was not

that sort of girl at all, and he had only too much reason to fear that his absence would cause her no regret. But there was truth in what Alec said; and by leaving Arbroath he might at least make a position worthy of her.

' Gae you hame, laddie,' Alec concluded, 'an' I'll juist bring alang the siller to you.'

So Andrew returned to his home, and shortly after Alec came in with the money. But Andrew would not accept the loan then; and Alec, not reluctantly, put the bag again into his pocket.

A thought had occurred to Rayne; and as soon as Alec had gone he took down his fowling-piece from the rack over the door and examined it, to see if it would not be possible to sell it, and so raise money enough for a trip to Nottingham the next day. His heart was hopeful for the future

as he mounted on a chair to replace the
piece; but as he lifted it he stumbled and
fell to the ground. The gun, partly in
the rack, slipped and, going off, lodged a
bullet in the back of his neck.

From that day Andrew had hovered
between life and death, unconscious of the
feeling against Alec his accident had roused,
until this morning, when Dr. Murdoch had
asked him if he could account for the
wound that had so nearly been mortal.
His explanation was altogether satisfactory,
and the only result of the accident was to
determine Rayne to give up his hope of
winning Alison in favour of the doctor, to
whom he owed his life. When he heard
how much was due to Murdoch's skill, all
unconscious of Alison's love for him, he
resolved to leave the town without making
any further effort to win her.

Alison, meanwhile, ignorant of the web

fate was spinning round her, was setting out with May for the proposed walk to the Redhead. The day was glorious—a perfect spring morning, frost on the ground and blue overhead—and there was a fine exhilaration about her companion that May, jealously observant, attributed to a wrong cause.

'Of course she is thinking of Dr. Murdoch!' May said scornfully to herself. 'I suppose by this time she has quite persuaded herself that he is in love with her!'

She tossed her pretty head and became oblivious of the beauty round her. Nothing so excited May's happiness as the attentions of a gentleman, and she was unable to realise that mere sympathy with Nature could bring (as perhaps it could not—who can tell?) such brightness to Alison's cheek, such sparkle to her eye. She watched her furtively, and in a few minutes decided on a course of action that would reverse their positions, and make Alison as jealous and as far removed from Dr. Murdoch as May was feeling herself at that moment. She was too diplomatic to show her hand at the outset of the game, and she assumed a merriment and a sympathy with Alison that she was far from feeling.

They were out on the cliffs, and had passed the Mermaid's Kirk. Alison was in keen enjoyment of the clouds massed on the horizon, white and shining above the snow-covered peaks of the distant mountains.

There were no flowers in bloom on the cliffs, except here and there where a patch of bright gorse lit the close herbage that in a few months would be embroidered by the sea-daisy and white campion, the blue-bell and dwarf-heather, and all the variegated blossom that smiles on the cliff-paths in the summer-time. Yet there was no lack of colour now in this bright atmosphere, for the seaweed on the rocks below was touched by the sun to warm golden-brown; and the red sandstone was purple and grey, and varied with the dark tones of age.

Out by the Bell Rock the fishing-boats were just visible, the white sails looking like wings of a flight of sea-birds spread a moment on the water; while on the horizon rose the lighthouse like a tower of gleaming porphyry. On all the northern coast no fairer sight than this could be seen, and Alison felt a proud sense of possession in the beauty round her.

'The innumerable laughter of the sea,'

she said, aloud, as she paused to look round her. May glanced up in bright sympathy. After all, it is not worth while fearing one's opponent when one holds the ace of trumps.

'That's pretty, Alison; poetry seems the proper thing for the sea, doesn't it?'

To a certain type of mind the platitude is as natural as the epigram is to another!

Alison looked down at May in friendly amusement. After the living reality of thought called forth by her mill-life; after Jeanie's originality and the daring humour of Liz, May's commonplaceness was novel and refreshing.

'I don't think it is exactly *pretty*,' she said. 'The laughter of the sea always reminds me of the laughter of a man whose eyes are heavy with tears. That was the meaning Kingsley gave that line.'

'Yes,' May cried, with ready and unexpected comprehension, 'I know what you mean. Dr. Murdoch laughed so when he told us his mother was dead.'

Her voice sank, and she looked up to Alison with eyes full of sorrowful sympathy. But Alison was not to be beguiled into soberness on this day. Life flowed in too swift a current in her veins, the sky was too blue, the earth too glad for sorrowful memories. And yet, though she banished the thought, her mind flew to the promontory north of Lunan Bay, where the little burial-ground of St. Skae's in its pathetic loneliness was sending its sombre message across the bright waters.

It was a beacon for sailors; and Alison had often thought of the beautiful fitness there was in those desolate graves guiding the mariners to safety; the dead beckoning the living to the quiet haven where is shelter from the storm of life. But she would not be dismal on a day like this, and with a humorous association of ideas she began to tell May about the dead monks haunting the Abbey House.

Alison's comical story diverted May, and by the time they passed the Mason's Cave she was in restored good humour. She slipped her arm within Alison's, and dropped her voice to a confidential tone.

'Dr. Murdoch took me home last night, you know. He was *so* kind and attentive!'

'He is always that,' Alison said, practically.

'Oh, but he was specially kind last night! Alison, will I tell you a secret?'

Alison looked down in surprise at the low, significant tones, and her curiosity was roused by May's conscious face and averted eyes.

'If you can trust me with it!' she said, not dreaming that May's secret, told in that glorious sunshine, would throw a dark shadow on her own life.

'Well, darling, if I tell you, you must promise not to let a living creature know, for it is quite a secret. Dr. Murdoch and I are engaged—at least, not exactly engaged, but there is an understanding. There has been one for months, and when we are married father will give up the practice to him. Of course,' she continued hurriedly, not glancing, as she played her trump-card, at Alison, 'it is a splendid arrangement for John—Dr. Murdoch; it secures a good position for him without any outlay, for he could not afford to buy a practice like this for himself. Even if he did not care for me, he has too much sense to lose a chance like this.'

After this exceedingly prosaic speech May hung her head modestly; but Alison received the secret in silence, and something prevented May from asking for her congratulations.

'Do you know Miss Mansel?' she asked, a moment later.

'Do you mean Miss Mansel of Woodlands, or her pretty niece?'

'You'll know whom I mean fast enough when I tell you the story. She's not nice at all, and she nearly did the doctor a great injury the other day. She spread a report that he was paying her attentions, and people believed it. He lost a good many patients in the better houses, and he was cut by everybody, till father contradicted the report.'

'But why? Miss Mansel is a very nice girl—pretty, well-educated, and a lady. Why shouldn't he marry her?'

May was delighted that Alison had fallen into the trap set for her, and had hit upon the wrong lady. She shrugged her shoulders.

'Oh, she may be all that; but you know

she worked in a mill before they came into
all that money; and if he had married her
he would have been ruined professionally,
for no nice people would have associated
with them. Besides,' and May's voice expressed the high moral tone of her mind,
'he is virtually engaged to me, and no
honourable man would break off an engagement for a mere passing fancy. It
would kill me, I think,' she concluded
pathetically.

'Dr. Murdoch is not likely to do anything dishonourable,' said Alison a little
coldly, feeling that May need not have
alluded to the mill in that manner. May
caressingly pressed the arm she held.

'I am so glad you think so, darling.
Do you know, Alison, I had begun to be
the least bit jealous of you?'

Alison looked down at May's bright face,
and smiled bitterly.

'You need not have feared, May. Love is not for me; besides, I have done my loving.'

Having had eighteen years' experience of life to guide her, Alison believed she was speaking the truth. May, equally well versed in human nature, accepted the statement.

'Darling,' she said, sympathetically, 'won't you tell me all about it?'

For an instant Alison was silent, thinking how all these weeks Andrew had sent no word of love to her; how she had been denied admittance to the house by his mother, and how the story of his love for her was as though it had never been.

It is strange what an attraction a love-story has for a woman. Her interest in May's secret had caused Alison to forget her own grief; but now, when, in studiously careless tones, and with her usual smile, she told May that she had won a good man's love, she felt as though she too were laughing, while for anguish her eyes were streaming with tears. A girlish weakness to let May know that she, also, had been loved—that the despised mill-girl could win, as well as Dr. Lindsay's daughter, the love of an honourable man—had induced her to tell May this much. But she said nothing of her own love for Andrew. She did not know that the bitter laughter on her lips had not been called forth by the remembrance of her slighted love, but by the story May had so artlessly confided to her!

CHAPTER XII.

ALISON'S HOPE.

THEY had reached Auchmithie by this time, and the two girls paused on the edge of the cliff overlooking the village.

The shallow waters of a little burn had cut for themselves a deep channel; and across the brook the houses of the village were perched on the brae like a cluster of dark-winged gulls on some steep cliff-side.

An air of antiquity and artistic decay hung about the place, and the modern hotel that stood scornfully looking down at the cottages huddled together about it seemed strangely out of keeping with the character of the village.

Away from the time-stained walls and moss-grown tiles of the cottages, the trim coastguard station kept a friendly eye on the white sands of the beach where the boats were drawn up, their gaily-painted hulls and tall masts showing to advantage in the foreground of the dark cliff.

The girls crossed the burn, and, after toiling up the brae, passed slowly down the long street, gazing with interest at the fishwives; picturesque and quaint figures in their short serge petticoats and bright-coloured bodices. The fishers, too, sitting stolidly at the doors sorting the lines for the fishing, were attractive in their rude reserve and strength; but the girls felt that they had come into another world from the brisk life of Arbroath, and had been transported away from mills and

shops into a life that was nearer to the
heart of Nature. Here there was struggle,
too; but it was silent and reserved, and
strong in a peace unadorned by the passing forms of art and civilisation, and there
was a rude dignity in the repose of the
villagers.

Alison and May, passing down the
street with their bright faces and eager
eyes, were incongruous figures in a scene
where everything seemed old-world and
restful; as though life in the little village
had been hushed to sleep by Time's hand
centuries before, and had remained sleeping still. Even the children, who paused
in their task of picking mussels and clean-
ing haddocks to stare at the visitors, had
about them an air of mature industry and
knowledge of life that was very pathetic.
No merry laugh echoed from them; now
and then a woman would call shrilly to

any loiterer in her task; otherwise the
work went on in quiet, busy monotony.
But the sun smiled down upon the scene
as though it would throw some brightness
into the lives of these silent, struggling
men and women.

Alison would have lingered in the village, but May hurried her on—her dainty
nose perked up suggestively—and would
not let her slacken her pace till they were
well away from the houses and on the
road to Ethie. Then the brightness of
the day began to take effect on May as
well as Alison. She had relieved her
mind, and was enjoying the happiness resulting from an unencumbered intellect.
Had she not concocted that plausible little
story of Dr. Murdoch's relations to her,
Alison would not have revealed her own
secret, and she would have known nothing of the rival Dr. Murdoch had in

another man for whom, she suspected, Alison cared a great deal. How bright the day was !

May was not given to introspection. It did not occur to her that she had been guilty of a base meanness in deceiving her friend. There was a little truth in her story—it was not utterly untrue. This falsehood was no empty bag that must collapse inevitably ; there was enough truth in it to enable it to keep the perpendicular, and make a fair show of being full. She could not be accused of fabricating the whole thing, for Dr. Lindsay had really suggested to Dr. Murdoch that he should marry his daughter and take the practice. May knew this, for she had been in the room, hidden behind the heavy curtains, and had heard the whole conversation. Also, there had been some gossip about the doctor's attentions to old Miss

Mansel, who was rich and twice his age; but May did not tell Alison that this report was groundless, and that Dr. Murdoch had not jumped at her father's suggestion.

'A lie that is half a lie is ever the worst to fight.' The line flashed through her mind, but she carelessly dismissed it.

This story that she had told Alison had done no one any harm. In fact, it had done good by changing the aspect of affairs, and showing her how little cause she had to dread Murdoch's admiration for Alison.

How lovely the clouds were; each a bank of soft snow flushed to tenderest rose-pink by the sun beginning now to slant westward. Clearly it would have been a mistake to have let herself remain in ignorance of Alison's real feelings towards the doctor. May prepared to enjoy nature to the utmost.

They were through the wood now, and

again they turned seaward, and passed down the field to the Redhead, the highest point of cliff along the coast.

They startled the gulls by their voices, and the birds rose and skimmed above their heads, filling the air with their harsh, discordant cries. A peregrine falcon wheeled overhead, and the girls paused to watch its flight before they retraced their steps to the house where they would take lunch. On the way home Alison tried to rouse herself from the depression that had fallen upon her since that allusion to Andrew, and soon she was able to respond with her usual gaiety to May's talk.

'By the way, Alison,' May said, after a time, 'did Dr. Murdoch ever find out where he had seen you? You remember that absurd notion of his about having met you in some grand dress somewhere, don't you? Did you ever explain it to him?'

'No. He has asked me about it. Perhaps he dreamed it!'

May gave Alison a keen glance, and saw that she had changed colour as she spoke.

'I suspect a mystery there!' she said, shaking her head wisely. 'Don't you intend to explain it, Alison?'

'There is nothing to explain,' Alison said, quickly. 'I am going to sing now, so don't talk, May.'

Before May could protest Alison began to sing, and her wild song ringing across the water caused the fishermen in the distant boats to respond with answering chorus.

'After all, May,' Alison said, brightly, 'it is worth while being cheerful for other people's sake. Even though we sing through our tears some echo of the song will reach us from hearts that it has cheered.'

'Yes,' May said, piously; 'and singing

always sounds so well across the water, especially by moonlight. But we should hasten, Alison, for the trap was to meet us at Auchmithie.'

Late that night, when all the house was quiet, Alison stood at her window gazing out at the Abbey walls, rising dim and ghostly in the shadowy midnight. How silent and deserted everything seemed! How still and cold, save for the stars shining overhead and the breeze stirring in the leafless branches of the trees! She could hear the distant murmur of the waves in the silence, and her thoughts went away beyond the sea and beyond the stars to Jeanie. Where was she then? Had she reached home, and was the darkness light about her?

How far away from her seemed her old life now! Jeanie and Liz and Andrew— all had passed completely away from her;

she was in another sphere from theirs.

It was only three months since she had been overwhelmed with grief at Jeanie's death and Andrew's danger, and now she could think calmly of both. Andrew had refused to see her when she had called at the house; but even this act had lost the sting it had had for her.

She leaned her head against the window-pane, and wondered how it was his silence and coldness had not grieved her more. She was conscious that she did not wish to return to her old position as Andrew's sweetheart; and yet, if she could have gone to him and told him that she had once cared for him, her mind would have been at rest. He thought her disloyal to him. He had given her up easily, believing she cared for Dr. Murdoch, and it would have comforted her to have told him that he had been mistaken.

But *was* he mistaken?

Suddenly in the darkness her face burned at the memory of the look she had surprised on the doctor's face the day before, and she began to tremble at the joy that thrilled through her in sharp throbs. It was impossible that he could love her! She would just as soon expect the big, round O in the Abbey wall to come down and form one of the letters of the word *hero*, as that Dr. Murdoch should care for her. It was equally impossible that she could love him! She had been so certain that she loved Andrew that she had never distrusted her liking for Murdoch. Alison would as soon have thought of falling in love with St. Tammas himself as with the young doctor!

And yet what did all this sweet trembling mean if she did not love him?

She pressed her face to the window-pane and looked out at the still, cold stars; but they gave no answer to the question in her wistful eyes. She began to think over the past in its association with him. His goodness to Jeanie and herself at the time of the accident had first called forth her gratitude. She could never forget that long night of anxiety when his presence at Jeanie's bedside had been such a comfort to her.

There was another incident of that night which she had altogether forgotten, but now it returned to her with a stinging, burning shame; for on that night she had kissed the doctor's hand! The memory was torture, and her face grew white as she recollected what she had done. What must he have thought of her? How could she have done it? She bent her head and sobbed in tearless, passionate misery at the recollection of her unmaidenly act.

Poor Alison! Yet there is often an element of the comic in the truest pathos. Nature refuses to weep in unmitigated sorrow, and is very ready with her rainbow smile after a tearful outburst. And Alison's grief had its humorous side, for, at the moment when she was upbraiding herself for that immodest caress, Dr. Murdoch was stroking the hand she had kissed, and dwelling on the act with tender satisfaction!

Rayne had told him that day that he had nothing to keep him in Arbroath, and was going away to Nottingham as soon as his convalescence was assured; and Murdoch was a happy man. He gazed triumphantly into the future, seeing the girl he loved coming to him with the love-light in her eyes through the darkness of her cloudy hair. Alas! poor Murdoch. He was nearing the end of his happiness; and no warning voice told him that the darkness through which Alison would come to him was not her own loveliness, but the shadow of a crime.

Alison, meanwhile, was full of a bitter despair. She knew now that she loved the doctor as she had never loved Andrew; and she knew also that love was hopeless. The words that May had said to her that day beat with remorseless iteration in her ears.

'She worked in a mill, and if he had married her he would have been ruined professionally. . . . He is pledged to me, and no honourable man would break off an engagement for the sake of a mere passing fancy. It is a splendid arrangement for Dr. Murdoch, as it secures a good position for him without any delay, for he could not afford to buy a practice for himself.'

The words beat on her ears like the knell of doom, and she sobbed aloud, for they set a seal upon her happiness. Even though the doctor cared for her, his honour forbade him to declare his love, for he was pledged to May. And though he were honourably free she could not allow him to sacrifice his position and prospects to her. If he would be ruined professionally by a marriage with Miss Mansel, who was an heiress, though she had worked in a mill, what would follow if he married the portionless orphan of a sea captain, Alison, of the Ward Mill?

Alison was too sensible and practical to suppose that her residence in the Abbey House made any vital difference in herself. As a millworker she would not have dreamed of a marriage with the doctor; and, she said to herself, if Alison, of the mill, had been unworthy to be his wife, her altered position would not remove the unworthiness.

She and Jeanie, with many other girls, had proved that a woman could be as pure and true, noble and beautiful, in the mill as in the most refined and sheltered home. If the mill girl were unfit to mate with the doctor, Mrs. Urquhart's companion was equally unfit, and her love was hopeless. She was right enough in her argument, this proud young Alison, who would owe nothing to artificial circumstances; but then she did not know that it was as a mill girl that Dr. Murdoch had loved her first.

She was not perfect by any means, and her heart was full of hard thoughts against fate that had spoiled her life, and against May, who had won a happiness she did not value.

Only that morning the words, used in

another sense, had passed her lips, 'Love
is not for me—I have done my loving.'
She had said them quietly, thinking of
Andrew; but now she said them again
bitterly, as she thought of Dr. Murdoch,
and realised how much she lost in losing
his love. A lonely, loveless life in the
future was before her. With a dumb
agony in her heart she looked out at the
dim, remote stars; and as she looked up
she began to see lights flashing from the
future that had looked so dark. Her
happy home, her own gifts of musical
voice and artistic fingers, her influence
over the mill girls, the brightness she
could bring into their lives—all these
were stars that would light the path that
had seemed so black before her.

She was rich in friends; and this love
that had come to her with such sad attend-
ants of pain and anguish would be a price-

less possession to ennoble her whole life. Her love was hopeless, but she would strive to make herself worthy of Dr. Murdoch's love.

Then she gave a little guilty start, for she had unwittingly changed the motive that had always before inspired her efforts. Hitherto her one aim had been to follow her father's example—now it was to be worthy of Dr. Murdoch's love.

Ah, Mrs. Urquhart's prophecy had had a speedy fulfilment.

Alison had found another hero !

CHAPTER XIII.

AN EXPEDITION TO DUNDEE.

'It's very kind of you to come in and see me, Mrs. Lindsay,' said Mrs. Urquhart; 'I am getting so used to having Alison with me—it is more than a year now since she came to me, you know—that I miss her when she's away only an hour or two.'

'I know that,' chirped the little woman; 'and I would not have kept her, only Dr. Murdoch was in, and wanted Alison and Mr. James to stay for a game of nap—he's such a man for a game! I left the four of them playing, and came off to sit with you.

By the way, are you sure your nephew isn't in love with Alison?'

'I'm sure he isn't, Mrs. Lindsay. I'm afraid he hasn't enough wit to do anything so sensible, poor lad!'

'You would like it, then?'

'For my own sake and for his; but he is not good enough for Alison.'

'Very few are that,' Mrs. Lindsay said quickly. 'She's a real bonnie, sensible lassie, and as good as she is pretty. It isn't every man I'd like to see her marry. How would you like Dr. Murdoch, now?'

Mrs. Urquhart looked up sharply.

'Well, there's no one I'd give her up to so soon as the doctor. He's a fine lad, and they're well suited to each other, but he likes some one else.'

'Good gracious, Mrs. Urquhart! You don't believe that mad story about old Miss Mansell?'

'Not a bit of it. But there's another lady: he told me so himself.'

Mrs. Lindsay's thoughts flew to May.

'I hope it's not my May,' she said, sharply.

'And why not, Mrs. Lindsay? Where would you find a better husband for her? Murdoch is a man in a thousand!'

'That's just what I think. I love him as if he were my own son, and I'm sure I wish he were. But May is not the wife for him —though I say it.'

'May is a bonnie lassie, and I'm very fond of her. I'll not hear you say anything against her,' Mrs. Urquhart said.

'I daresay not;—she's a true woman, full of nonsense and flirtation, and lads and dress. I'm sure she doesn't get it from me; but her father spoils her, aud gives her her own way in everything. Ah, Mrs. Urquhart! I've been so busy telling other women their duty that I've had no time to look after my own bairn!'

There was a touch of real feeling under the light words that Mrs. Urquhart detected.

'Never fear!' she said, kindly. 'May will make a fine woman yet. There's good stuff in her under her frivolity. How does Liz get on with her?'

'Oh, well enough; they are both fond of dress and lads. Liz is getting quite a fine lady now, and she talks English as well as May, without costing what May did at her London school. I have to be very plain with Liz, for she is always ready to gossip with Dr. Murdoch, and wastes her time whenever he gives her an opportunity. But I'm gossiping myself, and I wanted to have a sight of Alison's picture.'

'You will find it in the studio, Mrs. Lindsay. It is nearly finished now, and Tibbie Mearns makes a bonnie picture.'

Mrs. Lindsay went into the next room to inspect Alison's canvas. The subject was a simple cottage interior, the attic in which the girl had lived. There was the window with the rose on the sill, and the lilac tree outside; there were the bare boards and the rough white-washed walls; and rudely sketched in the foreground was the figure of a millworker, Tibbie Mearns, sitting wearily in her chair.

The little bare room, the single cup and saucer on the table, the small bed, the weary girl in the chimney corner, all spoke eloquently of the lonely life of the majority of mill girls.

Mrs. Lindsay thought of the demoralising hand-to-mouth life of so many of them: of the sacrifice of proper food for an improper finery: of the low standard of morals that spread like a festering sore through the factory community, and her heart swelled with pity for these girls who had never had a chance of anything higher or better. Their mothers had worked in the mills before them; they themselves. would be—God help them!—the mothers of another generation of millworkers. If nothing was done to alter the existing wrongs that pressed upon them, where would the degeneration of life and morals end?

She thought of her own May, and the mother in her rose up in strong pity for the lonely girls who, like Tibbie Mearns and Bell Macniel, were motherless. Who could save them from the almost certain temptations to which they were exposed? The wonder was that any girls could live the life, and yet remain the pure and beautiful women that so many were! Yet what could she do?—a single woman against a whole system—a solitary worker in the midst of the great evils of poverty and misery!

Mrs. Lindsay affected to despise women; and in her daily life her sharp professional manner and readiness of resource had earned her the credit of possessing masculine strength and self-reliance. But she left Alison's studio a typical woman; one of those whose blood rises at the tale of a sister's suffering, whose tears fall at the recital of the doom to which hundreds of innocent girls are born, and yet who stop short at indignation and pity, and never lift a hand to alter the existing conditions of life.

Happily for the mill workers of Arbroath, Alison had been among them, one of themselves, and now she was to help in accomplishing what Mrs. Lindsay with all her strength of will was impotent to undertake. But when she came home that evening she looked more like the very human girl she was than like the heroine of a great reform; and Mrs. Urquhart was troubled at the sight of her pale face.

'Alison, dearie,' she said, 'what is ailing you? You are no yourself, my bairn. You are doing too much.'

'No,' Alison said, quietly, 'I like work, and I don't get too much now.'

'But you should take a rest. You are not over-strong, and Dr. Murdoch says you are doing too much.'

Alison winced at the name, and Mrs. Urquhart's keen eye caught the change in her face.

'Yes, the doctor came in to-day. He wants you to go with him to Dundee to-morrow to see a picture they are exhibiting just now. Did he say anything to you about it?'

'No; but I don't wish to go, maimie;

you can't spare me a whole day, you know! Besides, it is Tibbie Mearns's wedding to-morrow night.'

'That won't hinder your going to Dundee in the morning! And as for me, I must learn to want you, my bairn, for some one will take you away from me altogether some day.'

A red flush swept over Alison's face, and her eyes were full of pain.

'Never! never!' she almost sobbed, covering Mrs. Urquhart's hand with kisses; 'I shall never leave you, maimie, I'm to be your bairn always!'

'No, no; I hope not. I want to see you happily married before I'm away. Alison, I'll tell you a secret. I was wishing Dr. Murdoch would grow to like you, but he has seen some one else already.'

'Yes,' Alison said, with a quick shiver, 'I know.'

'You know? Who told you?' Mrs. Urquhart asked jealously.

'May Lindsay—long ago—in confidence,' Alison answered hoarsely.

'Ah, yes! May wouldna keep it to herself, thoughtless lassie. And there is no one you would care for, my bairn?'

'No,' she whispered, for tears were threatening to betray her.

'Well, well, the right man will come some day. And meanwhile you have plenty to occupy you. The mill, the Guild, your painting and singing, and the love of a poor old woman like me.'

Alison kissed her softly, and Mrs. Urquhart went on diplomatically:

'And you will just go to Dundee with the doctor to-morrow; the change will do you good. He is to call for you at twelve. You will go, dearie?'

'Yes,' Alison said; but she knew there

would be no pleasure for her in the expedition.

However, the next day was gloriously fine—more like July than April—and Alison, in spite of herself, was in her happiest mood. She determined to forget May, and to give herself up to the gladness of being with the doctor for one short day. She would owe the day's happiness to him, as she already owed the best things of life to his influence. For had he not raised her life to a higher level of thought, given it a larger wealth of significance, and taught her a deeper experience—the experience of what is fine and noble that a sorrow worthily borne brings to every soul?

There was nothing in her companion to counteract the brightness of the morning. The doctor looked like a schoolboy out for a holiday, or like a man on his honeymoon, and she could not help smiling in sympathy with his radiant face. But she was shy, too; and, strangely enough, the more perceptible her shyness became the more delighted he looked, for it was a good sign that his suit would progress favourably.

How ridiculously joyful he was—how wickedly triumphant he felt that he had induced Alison to go up alone with him to Dundee! He had kept the expedition a secret from May, and secrecy lent an additional piquancy to the excursion; so, in the highest spirits, he laughed and chatted and kept Alison amused until they reached the gallery where the picture was on view. There was a large crowd before it, and they sat down to wait an opportunity of inspecting it closely. There were criticisms to be heard on all sides, and the doctor looked smilingly at Alison when two ladies sat down beside them and began to discuss the picture. By-and-by his own name caused him to raise his eyebrows in amused surprise.

'Don't you think that figure to the left very like Dr. Murdoch?'

'No, it's not handsome enough.'

Murdoch looked delightedly at Alison, and she smiled at his pleasure in the flattery. What a boy he was, after all!

'He is a very clever fellow,' the lady continued; 'the doctor, I mean. What a pity he is going to marry that girl!'

'I don't think so. She is very pretty, and of course Dr. Murdoch will step into the practice.'

'Oh, I don't mean May Lindsay! They say he has jilted her for Alison Dean.'

'Alison Dean? Nonsense! He knows better than to marry a mill-girl; his family would never consent to it—they are very exclusive. This Alison is quite a low girl; he would never marry her. But he has no idea of doing so; it is she that is trying to entrap him into an engagement!'

Alison could bear it no longer. She looked imploringly at Dr. Murdoch, whose face had set with a sternness she had never seen on it before. He was pale with pity for her, and he rose with a sudden movement that silenced the speakers, and made them turn with horrified amazement to the two they had been discussing.

'I must trouble you to let me pass,' he said, pushing a way through the crowd for Alison. She followed mechanically— her one thought being the necessity of remaining alone with him after the conversation they had overheard. To have heard it at any time would have been hard, but in his presence the words had carried a tenfold sting. They might ignore the words, but each knew that the other had heard, and the day was spoiled for both.

'Let us look at the other pictures,' she said hastily, wishful to break the silence between them. He did not glance at her, but he answered readily.

'Yes; come and see this one—it reminds me of the sculptor Thorwaldsen, who wept because he could find no flaw in his work.'

He led her into another room, and Alison stood gazing at a little water-colour.

'You see,' he continued, 'there is enough of the faulty here to give the artist's genius that growth and aspiration that is the surest test of greatness. If this picture had been perfect I should have despaired of his future—level perfection means decay and death. Everything great is more or less imperfect, and this man will be one of our greatest artists.'

He was talking to give her time to recover herself, and she was grateful to him for it.

'Your criticism reminds me of some verses I heard once,' she said :

> ' When the current of youth is strong
>   Our rhythmic thoughts flow free ;
> But the river must cease its song
>   As it nears its home, the sea :
> And we reach the results of life
>   With a hush of heart and brain,
> That is mute regret for the strife
>   We shall never know again.
>
> Although we may conquering rise,
>   We shall look with yearning sweet
> And a smart in the sun-dimmed eyes,
>   To days when we knew defeat ;
> And the crown of the life's success
>   We shall wear with longing vain,
> For the years of our loneliness,
>   And the joy that we thought was pain.'

Alison's voice trembled at the last line, and the doctor said kindly,

'Well, now, what do you say to going to Lamb's for some lunch?'

Evidently both intended to ignore the subject that was nearest their hearts.

Like a hot iron the words were burning

into the girl's consciousness: 'He would never marry her; it is she who is trying to entrap him into an engagement.' And the stinging shame she felt in his presence was threatening to break down her self-control altogether.

But the responsibility of her woman's nature was upon her. Whatever she felt must be hidden from him, and she must go to Lamb's and laugh and jest and make merry over the meal, just as though she were a careless, happy girl, and not a pain-stricken woman.

We can all remember times like this when the very depth of our anguish nerved us to hide it from all curious eyes. Alison being a woman, succeeded in dissembling her feelings better than the doctor; and it was owing to her efforts that they got through the next hour without any further awkwardness.

Murdoch was full of sympathy for her, and could not help showing it; but under his tender solicitude he was recklessly happy, for by and by he was going to take the sting from the words, and prove to the girl that they were not worth a thought.

'There is a train to Arbroath in a quarter-of-an-hour; shall we take that?' Alison asked, looking up from her plate when lunch was over.

His face fell. Was she, then, going to give him no opportunity of telling the story he had come out to tell her?

'So soon?' he asked. 'Are you anxious to return?'

'Yes; Tibbie Mearns is to be married to-night. I have promised to go to the marriage.'

'So have I!' he said, gaily, for his fertile mind had hit on a plan by which he should still have an uninterrupted *tête-*

à-tête with Alison. 'Well, let us take this train, if you like.'

Alison was glad to find herself in the railway-carriage; and she leaned her head on the cushion and closed her eyes, thankful that the doctor's *Scotsman* relieved her from the duty of talking to him.

'We get out here,' said his quiet voice after a time, and she opened her eyes, and in some confusion was handed from the carriage by Murdoch. It was not till the train had begun to move that she noticed that they had not alighted at Arbroath, but at Elliot; and she glanced enquiringly at her companion. He was very grave, and he scarcely smiled when he answered the look.

'It is such a beautiful afternoon; I thought you might like to walk home along the shore.'

It was too late to demur to the arrangement, and she followed him in silence from the platform; and in silence began the two miles' walk along the level sand.

There were no rocks between Elliot and Arbroath, no cliffs or elevated land; but the shore had a quiet beauty of its own, and the waves came rolling in in stately ranks and orderly sequences. A soft haze hung over the sea; and a bank of white clouds before her recalled to Alison's memory the walk with May to the Redhead a year ago, 'the innumerable laughter of the sea,' and the answering laughter in her heart when she had heard that Dr. Murdoch was engaged to May.

She turned to look at the hills behind her. A soft, purple light of sunset enfolded them, and they faded away into a soft purple sky. She could scarcely tell where the hills ended and the sky began; but the pearly, indefinite atmosphere seemed to her like the smile of the dying day—peaceful and sad and tender, with a vague suggestion in it of the nightfall.

There were no gleaming white sails of distant fishing-boats to-day—the deserted sea stretched away to the horizon; and the waves lapped the shore with a strange, beautiful monotony of sadness in their deep voices. Over everything brooded a sorrowful wistfulness, and Alison turned with dim eyes to the long stretch of sand before her.

Neither she nor Murdoch had spoken since they left the station, and, wondering at his silence, she glanced up at him. Then she put out her hand with a shrinking gesture.

'Oh, Dr. Murdoch, please don't!'

But he took her hand and held it fast, drawing her unresisting to him.

'Alison, my darling, you *must* hear me! You must hear me now, for Alison, I love you!'

CHAPTER XIV.

' ALISON, I LOVE YOU!'

No life is perfect into which love does not enter; and yet the very spirit of love is sacrifice. It is only when the flower falls that its mission is fulfilled, and the perfume that lies in each rosy petal is scattered to give sweetness to many winds. Christ, as King of the Jews, would have ruled over a tiny empire; Christ, the type of sacrifice, is king wherever nature and love are found. It was because Alison's love for the doctor was so true that it appealed to her now as a sacrifice rather than as a joy, to be gathered and worn for herself only.

'Alison, I love you!'

How her heart thrilled at the words; and yet each one brought her a two-edged agony—the necessity of being deaf to them; and the knowledge that they were not the outcome of his love for her, but of the circumstances which had shamed her in his presence!

Oh, yes, she understood it well enough. Dr. Murdoch would display his generosity, and because she had been insulted before him, he would show her that he did not despise the mill-girl. He was ready to make any sacrifice to prove his regard for the 'girl of low birth.'

With all her ability Alison had no comprehension of the springs that move the masculine nature. Here she was dignifying Murdoch with the highest and most

exalted motives, when he had only been
actuated by the natural, and not at all
praiseworthy or uncommon one of wishing
to make the woman he loved his wife!

But there are some simple (and large-
faithed) souls who persist in crediting poor
humanity with god-like and heroic virtues;
and so long as they feel the stirrings within
them of divine and noble impulses, you
will not persuade them that their faith
in human nature is ill-founded. Though
the religion of humanity has not yet found
its reliable exponent, it is informed with
the true spirit of beauty and art, and is
pierced through with a mystery. A
mystery revealed now and again in a clear
light of sacrifice, by which we have glimpses
of noble souls struggling through the darkness after a solitary Figure toiling up a
cross-crowned height. And in spite of
pessimistic views of human nature, I assert

that no day of life passes without its Calvary and its victim.

Alison, walking along the level reach of sand, knew that the steep ascent of self-sacrifice was before her.

' Alison, I love you !'

He had drawn her to him, and now holding her hand passionately he waited for her next movement.

She became pale and cold, and dark rings gathered under her eyes as she stood mute in the silence broken only by the deep moaning of the sea. Then she gently withdrew her hands, and there was a look on her face that he had not expected to see. He had not fancied her averse to him. She had avoided him lately, and had been shy and distant with him, but Murdoch had been hopeful that these were signs that she was conscious of a special interest in him— and now !

He took her hand again, and he noticed that she did not shrink from his touch though her eyes were full of pain; and he determined that he would not give her up unless she told him that she loved another. He had lost his jealousy of Andrew since the lad had gone away to Nottingham; but now he began to fear that Alison's love for Rayne had survived his absence, and he determined to settle that matter before they reached Arbroath. He stooped and looked steadily and gravely into her eyes.

'Alison, tell me that you cannot love me!'

She could not meet his glance. Her eyes fell before the burning light of his; and she trembled, feeling that he could compel her to answer him even against her will.

His power was great over her; and even at this moment she was conscious of a subtle force drawing her irresistibly to him.

'She loved him! Oh, she knew now the difference between her love for Andrew and her love for Dr. Murdoch, and yet she must refuse him! For his own sake she must refuse him!

'Dr. Murdoch is not likely to do anything dishonourable,' she had said to May. And yet here he was declaring his love to her when he was virtually pledged to May!

But she understood that an impulse to honour her, to prove the falsity of the words they had heard, was the sole motive of his present action. Even Mrs. Urquhart knew of his engagement to May; and though he had been free, Alison could not allow him to be 'ruined professionally' for her sake—

'I love thee so much, dear, I cannot but leave thee.'

A line from one of her songs occurred to her while she trembled under his glance; but she must not let him see that she loved

him with all her heart, and that therefore
she must leave him.

She smiled bitterly to herself. Life had
again offered her its choicest gift. Love
had blossomed for her, and it was like the
anemone she had seen on the rocks at low
water—a brilliant, beautiful flower that
stung to agony the hand that plucked it.
The vision she had seen in the Abbey was
realised. The life of art and beauty was in
ruins round her, and nothing remained of
love but a grave!

'Tell me that you cannot love me,' Dr.
Murdoch said again, insistently.

She stood before him, blushing, conscious, shrinking, and he pitied her; but
he must have an answer to his question.
If it was impossible for her to love him, he
would not ask her to be his wife; but, if
there was hope for him, then, as he was a man,
he would win her! He almost crushed the

hand he held ; for he was no gentle wooer, and if he had lived a few centuries earlier he would not have stood there parleying with his lady-love, but would have carried her off bodily to his castle—where, no doubt, she would have been all the more devoted a wife to her headstrong, self-willed lover ; for a woman admires nothing so much in a man as the courage of conquest in life, in love, and in war.

'You *must* answer me !' he said, boyishly. 'You have no right to refuse to give me an answer !'

Then Alison looked up to him, with a world of anguish in her beautiful eyes.

'Don't ask me anything—don't! I can never be your wife !'

'But I *must* ask you to marry me! I am only a poor country doctor, and not a great match for any one. You might marry a richer man, but not one that would love you more than I !'

'I know that. Oh, Dr. Murdoch! you cannot think the—the money—would interfere—would make me—refuse you! I am only a mill-girl—not fit to be your wife.'

Her voice broke, and he interrupted her fiercely—

'You are not thinking of what that confounded woman said to-day? You can't believe there was any truth in what they were saying? A mill-girl! Hang it all! Don't you know that you are a hundred times too good for me? See here, Alison, there is only one thing that will make me give you up.—Do you love anyone—now —at this moment?'

Alison's heart gave a wild bound—could he not tell that she loved him? She bowed her head, unable to speak, while the red flush was crimsoning over her face.

Dr. Murdoch saw her confusion. He

never guessed that those red signals were hung out for him; and his face became still and cold.

'That fellow—Rayne?' he asked, setting his teeth closely.

Poor Alison! It was an added bitterness that Andrew's name should be mentioned at this moment. Her lips quivered, and she turned away her face to hide her emotion.

The doctor misunderstood the movement; and he felt the devil rise in him that he should be baulked of his desire by a man utterly unworthy of Alison. She with her splendid gifts, her refinement and culture, to sink to the level of a working man's wife?

The doctor cursed the mad folly that had induced him to labour night and day to save Andrew's life. Why in the world had he not left the man to Dr. Lindsay, to be killed or cured as Nature and fate ordained? So he thought, and his conceit was magnificent! Why had he saved him to come between himself and Alison? He laughed bitterly, conscious of his own presumption in claiming to dispense life and death.

'If a man is to live a thousand doctors won't kill him;' he had been used to say reassuringly to the friends of his patients; and he knew well enough that his own efforts had only been as instruments in a stronger hand. He deliberately took Alison's hand in his again.

'I am satisfied now,' he said rudely. 'But you owe me something, and I shall claim my debt.'

Alison stood frightened and wondering at his manner, while he drew off her glove and gazed at her, his face white with passion.

'You kissed my hand once,' he said slowly, 'and that kiss made me move heaven and earth to save Rayne's life— and now I shall take it back.'

Before she understood the words he raised her hand to his lips, and pressed a burning passionate kiss upon it.

'There, we are quits now!' he said roughly, letting her hand fall; and in another moment he was striding away from her along the sands.

Alison hid her face in her hands in a passion of weeping. Was this her hero? —this fierce, angry man, who had insulted her by that passionate act? She moaned at the humiliation he had put upon her, but his voice checked her sobs.

'I beg your pardon,' he began, 'I——'

He was beside her, and she lifted her face proudly, but her eyes fell at his quick cry:

'Oh, my darling, forgive me! I was mad, I did not know what I was doing. It was because I love you so. Oh, Alison, I have been hoping all these months you would be my wife! I loved you from the first day I saw you, and I meant to ask you to marry me when we went to Dundee to-day. You have not given me a chance before, you know; and I was mad when I knew there was no hope for me. Will you forgive me, and forget the whole thing?'

He was as boyish in his penitence as in his anger, and Alison could not but believe him. Her face became bright with hope. After all he had loved her as a mill-girl; he had meant to ask her to marry him before they had listened to the cruel words that had spoiled their day; he loved her! And though May Lindsay stood between them, still he loved her! She smiled through her tears as she answered:

'I have nothing to forgive. Let us forget everything that has occurred to-day. If anything has spoiled our pleasure, we can remember that "all that is great is imperfect."'

Her face was quivering, and she was not offended when he raised her hand reverently to his lips.

'Good-bye,' he said. 'God bless you!—you are a good woman!'

He strode away quickly, and then he turned to ask:

'Shall I see you to-night at Mearns's?'

'No,' Alison said, 'I am not going.'

CHAPTER XV.

THE STORM.

'It's a wild night for Tibbie's marriage,' said Mrs. Urquhart; 'I am glad you are not going, Alison. How high the wind is! I declare it makes me feel quite nervous.'

'I like it,' Alison said, 'though no one has more cause to fear a storm than I have. Still I would rather have a strong wind than a breeze any day.'

'The breeze belongs to comedy, the wind to tragedy. The one is a lyric, the other an epic,' the poet remarked.

'It is strange what poetry there is in sea and storm and sorrow and all the tragic forces of life,' Alison said, her thoughts reverting to her father who had lost his life in a storm.

'That is because pain is the fire-germ of all true poetry: "We learn in suffering what we teach in song."'

Dante Algernon's tone identified him with the makers of true poetry, and Alison was amused.

'I should like to witness a storm at night —that is, if I knew the boats were safe,' Alison said.

'Deary me, Alison, no Arbroath boats would go out in a night like this,' said Mrs. Urquhart.

'The *Saucy Tib* went out about six o'clock. I hope she got in before the wind rose,' said the poet.

'I hope so,' Alison said gravely. 'But Jim would scarcely be out in her on his wedding night.'

'No, I suppose not. Would you care to go down to the harbour by-and-by, Miss Alison? It's a fine sight to see the waves breaking over the wall.'

'Nonsense!' Mrs. Urquhart exclaimed. 'I will not hear of you taking the child out in all this storm.'

'I should like to go, maimie; I have never seen a high sea at night, and it is moonlight just now.'

Alison felt as though it would do her good to struggle with the storm, to fight with something! Oh, how she longed to get away to her own room, to be free to relax her composure and let her grief have its own way, instead of sitting there talking quietly about tragedy in the midst of her own tragic grief.

'If you go you must wrap a shawl round your head,' said Mrs. Urquhart, 'and put on a warmer dress, else you will take cold.'

'No fear of that, maimie, I am strong enough. Besides, I am used to being on the sea in rough weather. Father used to say I could pull a boat as well as any of the crew.'

Alison ran away, and soon returned equipped for her walk in thick ulster, and with a little shawl tied over her hair.

'It is no use being bothered by a hat,' she said; 'and now I feel as though I had been changed into a mill-girl again.'

Alison spoke lightly, but she half-wished that the words were true, and that she was once more the happy mill-worker, without any pressing misery of love to bear.

It was a terrible night. The wind came in wild gusts sweeping through the old archway of the Abbey Nook, almost taking Alison off her feet as she was driven before it. It was moonlight, as she had said;

and the clouds rushing wildly across the sky made it appear as though the moon was speeding through the dark, impelled onwards by the fierce storm.

Scarcely anyone was out of doors beside themselves, but when they reached the bottom of the High Street they saw that others were running down in the direction of the harbour. Some one shouted to the poet, but he could hear nothing for the wind roaring and shrieking round them. It was as much as he could do to help Alison along, and he was breathless with his exertions.

Alison fought the gale better than he did; and as she struggled with it she began to forget her trouble, and to feel light-hearted and buoyant, almost against her will. She lost sight of herself entirely when they reached the bridge over the Brothock, and she was face to face with an

excited group of fishwomen who stood
tearing their hair and wringing their hands.

The waves were breaking over the sea-
wall in great masses of rushing spray; and
above the roar of the waves and the noise
of the wind they heard the confused shout-
ing of men and the wild screaming of
women.

Some of them were on the protection-
wall yelling like mad things, and flinging
their arms out towards the dark and
swollen waves; and Alison called to the
poet that she would like to walk along the
wall. But when she ascended the steps
the wind and breaking sea drove her back,
and she was glad to get down and creep
under shelter of the wall to the end of the
pier, where a larger crowd was gathered.

As yet all the excitement was meaningless to them; but when they stood
beneath the tower and looked across the

furious waters they understood : for, struggling in the trough of the sea, seen now
and again as the moon sent fitful gleams
through the darkness, was a boat trying
to make for the harbour !

In such a sea it was impossible that it
should live ; and Alison's blood ran cold as
she realised that the men would go down
in the very presence of wife and friends.
Suddenly the wailing and shrieks of the
women seemed to fade into the distance,
for a hand grasped hers, and a girl's voice,
wild with impotent despair, rang in her
ears :

'Oh, Alison, it's the *Saucy Tib*! And
my Jim's aboard her!'

Alison turned quickly. It was Tibbie
Mearns, with wild eyes and hair loose and
streaming behind her, that had grasped
her hand.

'Oh, Tibbie! *Jim!*'

'Yes,' Tibbie shrieked, beside herself with excitement; 'they went out early, an' the gale wis on them a' in a minute, an' they've been beatin' aboot for hours an' canna get in! Oh, Alison! it's oor merriage nicht, an' there's nae chance for Jim!'

'But the lifeboat! the lifeboat!' Alison screamed. 'Why don't they get it out before it is too late!'

'The lifeboat's awa' i' Dundee! Oh, God, have mercy! have mercy!'

A terrible cry broke from her, for, as she spoke, the *Saucy Tib* was raised high on the waves and then tossed like a shell into the heaving depths. A cloud obscured the moon, and there was no light to tell if the boat had righted herself. Scream upon scream rang across the darkness—the wail of the wives and mothers whose sons and husbands were in the imperilled boat.

Some were on their knees praying in agonized accents of terror; some were leaping and screaming on the wall, with difficulty prevented from throwing themselves into the waves boiling below. Tibbie was clinging to Alison, and almost choking her; and everywhere there was the mortal despair of men and women powerless in the presence of death.

All at once there was a loud shout from the men straining their eyes into the black night; for there, on the crest of a wave, a dark object re-appeared, and they could see that the boat had not gone down.

'Light, light! Good Lord, send us light!' a woman's voice shrieked; and, as if in answer to her prayer, a swift ray shot from the moon down into the blackness of that awful sea. And then a wail of despairing horror rose up at the sight revealed by that sudden moonbeam. A boat, reversed, tossing helplessly on the waves, and four dark figures clinging to it in the madness of peril.

There had been five men in the boat. Where was the fifth?

The men were quite near to the harbour-mouth; near enough for their hoarse cries to be heard by the watching crowd.

'Thank God!' a woman sobbed, 'yon's my man; I ken his cry weel! He's no awa'!'

Alison had stood quietly holding Tibbie's hand; but now, when the cries of the drowning men mingled with the shrieks of those on the pier, she could bear it no longer. She sprang forward into the group of fishermen and sailors.

'Are you men?' she screamed. 'Will you see them die without moving a hand to help them?'

'The lifeboat's away, and there's no a

boat could live in a sea like that,' a man answered stolidly.

'But you must do something! They are doomed unless you help them!' she cried frenziedly.

'Na, na, lassie; we can dae naethin'. None but the Almighty can help them the noo!'

'But are there no ropes?—no way by which they could be got into harbour? Oh, you cannot let them die!'

'Gae you back oot o' this, lassie. Ye winna help 'em by greetin'; nae rope could drag her in, ye ken.'

'Yes, come away, Miss Alison; nothing can be done without the lifeboat,' said the poet, taking her arm to lead her away.

But Alison freed herself impatiently from his grasp and fell back among the women, while the poet suggested that they should try throwing the lead.

While they talked, suddenly there was
another wild cry and a confusion of shouts
as the crowd ceased watching the struggling boat, and rushed with one accord to
the pier-side, where they gazed down with
horror at a boat that—loosed from its
moorings and manned by one girl only—
was now making her way round to the
harbour mouth. The poet would have
sprung into it, but he was held back;
while Alison, tossed wildly though in the
comparatively quiet waters of the docks,
guided the boat skilfully round the
wall.

No one moved to prevent her; but, as
she passed the last flight of steps, a man
was seen to spring in beside her; and they
two, Alison and Dr. Murdoch, for it was
he, started together on their perilous
mission of succour.

In the intense excitement of seeing them

make their way through that raging sea the crowd became still.

Would they succeed? Could that frail craft with its crew—a foolhardy landsman and a helpless girl—weather the storm against which the well-trained sinews of five hardy fishers had been altogether powerless? The wild winds shrieked louder, and the black waves rose hungrily to meet the boat hurrying to an awful doom.

'Good God! It's twa mair lives thrown awa'!' said the harbour-master; 'but the lassie's mad, an' the doctor chap is madder to hae gane wi' her.'

'God bless her! God save her!' the women cried, who had friends clinging to the *Saucy Tib*; and they ceased their meaningless shrieks to scream wild prayers to the God of storms, in whose hands were the lives of those six imperilled souls.

The black clouds hurried up from the horizon as if to cast a veil over the tragedy to be enacted on the dark sea; but like a spirit of light the moon rushed before them to send its guiding rays to the plucky girl in the little boat.

Louder the wind shrieked and the waves roared, as, eager for their prey, they gathered round the tiny craft.

What hope was there for the brave spirits of those two? What hope for the waning strength of the four awaiting death? The clouds gathered nearer to the moon; but like a hunted thing she rushed before them still. And now the blinded eyes of the drowning men caught sight of the boat struggling to the rescue, and a hoarse cheer went up from them into the night.

It was heard by the group on the pier. Alison, too, heard it, and it gave her new courage. It was no easy task making way through those furious waters; and over and over again the boat was tossed far away from the *Saucy Tib.* Yet each failure only nerved Alison and Murdoch to fresh effort.

They were not so unfitted for the task as they appeared. In his early home on the Canadian coast Murdoch had been used to a sailor's life, and Alison could manage a boat with the skill of a trained seaman. In the midst of their peril each was cool and collected; trusting in God, themselves, and each other.

' Please God, we'll save them yet, Alison,' Murdoch shouted as a great wave tossed them away from the *Saucy Tib.*

' Ay,' Alison sang out; her clear voice ringing across the water to the perishing men. They shouted in response; and the girl bent to her oars with the strength of an indomitable courage.

Strung to a pitch of terrible intensity the crowd watched each movement from the pier.

There, close on the crest of a wave were the two boats; Murdoch clinging to the mast, a rope in one hand ready to throw to the fishermen. Now the rope bounds through the air, and—yes, it is caught!

No! it has fallen into the trough of the sea, and a wave has carried the two boats further apart. See, there she comes back! —the gallant little vessel, urged by Alison's iron muscles!—and the excitement on the pier becomes frantic.

'Cheer them!' cries the poet; and springing on the wall regardless of the drenching spray, he takes off his cap and cheers with all the strength of his lungs. The cheer is echoed by the crowd, and heard by those struggling for life; bringing its strange message of victory in the moment of defeat.

Up come the clouds black as ink, gaining steadily on the flying moon. O God, if darkness wins, what hope for those six souls!

Lights are flashing on the pier. They have brought out the rocket-apparatus, and now a rocket shoots up, trailing its red light defiantly across the angry clouds.

See, a wave has tossed the *Saucy Tib* right alongside the other boat! Now!

It is the only chance—one minute given for the men to quit their perilous position and spring into the rescuing boat.

Breathless—mad with excitement—those on the pier strain their eyes to watch. The next wave will separate the boats again! What are the men waiting for? Why don't they spring into the boat that brings a hope of life? The moment is an eternity; and the women leap frantically on the pier, calling with shrill voices to the *Saucy Tib*.

The two boats toss side by side. And now there rolls a heavy black wave towards them! Death advancing to claim the prey so nearly escaping him. Another moment!—another! O God!——

A wail of despair goes up from the excited watchers, for the clouds have closed over the moon, and a horrible darkness is on the face of the deep.

CHAPTER XVI.

THE RESCUE.

LIKE a sudden fierce spirit a rocket sprang into the darkness, swaying like a living thing before the wind. Its reflection in the water was like a rainbow overturned; and the rocket and its reflection made a golden circle in the black waves and dark sky. And there, passing through this ring of fire, seen an instant in its light, came a laden boat.

Cheer upon cheer rang out; and all along the pier to the bridge, where the women and children were gathered, it echoed, and was taken up and rang out again, till little children sleeping in their cots stirred, and slept again, to dream that angels were singing on land and sea of goodwill to men.

The plucky little craft came every moment nearer the harbour. Slowly, steadily she bore on, struggling with the waves, and only seen by those on the pier when the rockets cast their lurid glare over the water. Stout hands were pulling at the oars—hands of men into whose souls hope had entered; and a girl's clear voice was urging them to a deathless courage. On the pier hope sprang up as the boat rose on the edge of a wave, only to die again as she went down into the trough of the seething waters. But still the boat came on, and when the harbour mouth was reached, and the crowd surging over the edge of the wall caught sight of

six figures in her, a triumphant roar of
victory shouted defiance to the dark skies.
But four women, in an agony of terror,
were 'screaming and wringing their hands,'
each not knowing if it was her man that
would 'never come back to the town.'

Who shall describe the scene when one
by one the rescued men climbed the ladder
and reached the solid platform of the pier?
The rejoicings of the men, the tears and
kissings of the women! They were as
frantic with joy as before with terror; and
when Alison was helped up and stood,
drenched to the skin, before them, the
women fell on the ground and kissed her
feet and hands in an ecstasy of gratitude
to the girl who had saved their husbands'
lives.

Only poor Tibbie Mearns stood apart
with Bell Macniel, tearing her hair and

crying for her mother to come from her grave and comfort her. It was her bridal-night, but the sea had snatched the bride-groom from her; for her Jim was the one missing from among the rescued men. He had gone down within sight of home, within hearing of the cries of the girl he loved; and the dark waters had closed over his head on the night that should have witnessed his marriage. Alas for Tibbie! Equally dark were the waters under which she should sink to her early grave.

Dr. Murdoch clambered up the ladder after Alison. He was coolly unconcerned as ever, laughing and shaking hands with everybody as they clustered round him; but he bethought him of Alison, and turned from the crowd to look for her. She was with the poet, who had ready for her—he never explained where he had got it nor how he had kept it dry!—a large overcoat in which Alison was being wrapped.

'You're a wise man!' said Murdoch, heartily. 'Now, a good stiff glass of whisky and she will take no harm!'

Whisky was already circulating rapidly among the rescued fishers; but Dante Algernon produced a flask from his pocket, and Alison, much against her will, had to drink the dose the doctor poured out for her. But when she and her friends started to leave the pier there was an opposing shout; and before either she or Murdoch knew what was to happen next, each was lifted up, to be carried home in triumph on the shoulders of the fishermen!

It was useless for Alison to struggle and beg to be set down. The enthusiasm of the mob would not be satisfied without a

demonstration; so with torches alight
and a ringing chorus of cheers the procession formed to take them home.   Up Sea-
gate they went, Alison crying and laughing
at her strange position; up the High Street,
rousing the sleepy town by the strange
midnight hubbub.   At the old church
they paused to hear the chimes ring out
twelve o'clock, and then Murdoch called
to them to take the lassie to Springfield,
Dr. Lindsay's house.   The noise had aroused
Mrs. Lindsay, who kept late hours, and she
and May and Liz were at the door when the
procession stopped:

'It's a lassie half-drooned,' they told her;
and presently she saw Dr. Murdoch help-
ing a girl up the steps.

He paused at the door, and said a few
words to the crowd, thanking them for
their escort, and begging them to disperse

quietly; and then, accompanied by the poet, they went into the surgery.

'Mrs. Lindsay,' he said quickly, 'we want hot blankets and a big fire.'

'You shall have them,' she said, promptly, without asking who needed these things. 'Come away with me to the kitchen, my dear, and we'll have your wet things off and something hot for you.'

She hurried Alison away, and despatched May and Liz for dry clothes, while she made the girl drink a cup of coffee that was waiting for Dr. Lindsay. No one had any idea who the 'half-drooned lassie' might be, until May and Liz removed the shawl and coat, and Alison stood before them with dripping hair and garments.

'Alison!' the girls screamed.

'Oh, it's you, Alison?' Mrs. Lindsay said coolly. 'Well, as soon as you have these dry things on and are in your bed, you shall tell me what new prank you have been playing. May, go away upstairs with Liz, and draw your bed before the fire.'

With quick decision Mrs. Lindsay moved about, and in an inconceivably short space of time Alison found herself between warm blankets in May's bed. Then, when all the excitement was over, she began to cry hysterically.

'Very well,' said Mrs. Lindsay, 'you shall have a good cry and go off to sleep. Come away, girls; leave her alone, now, and let us see what Dr. Murdoch has to say about all this.'

May and Liz were on the *qui vive* with curiosity, and they were willing enough to follow Mrs. Lindsay to the surgery.

Dr. Murdoch was not there; he had gone home to change his wet clothes; but the poet gave them the story of Alison's heroism.

'Heroism?' said Mrs. Lindsay scornfully. 'Fiddlesticks! It was sheer foolhardiness. Alison has hurt her arm seriously, and I doubt it will never recover from the strain. I don't know what the men were about to let her do it.'

'No one saw her till she was nearly out of the harbour, and Murdoch risked his life in jumping into the boat. There were many there who would have been proud to go with her,' said the poet, thinking forlornly that he would have been in Murdoch's place had he not been held back.

'H'm! Yet none of them were willing to go without her! A piece of sentimental foolery, unworthy of Murdoch! If they had been lost, people would have had enough to say of reckless waste of life;

now they'll be praised to the skies because
Providence didn't punish them as they
deserved ! Heroism, forsooth !'

Nothing could exceed the scorn in the
little woman's voice, though her heart was
thrilling with admiration at the action she
condemned.

The poet bore her rebuke in silence,
and said nothing of the dry coat and the
whisky he had hurried away to procure
against the girl's return, if she ever came
back, from her perilous errand. It is true
' the world knows nothing of its greatest
men ;' and his own forced inaction had not
been without a heroic significance that
made him great in a true sense. His self-
control and thoughtfulness that night had
proved that Dante Algernon was capable
of higher things than even the publication
of a volume like ' Heart-Throes.'

By-and-by Mrs. Lindsay turned to him brusquely.

'My dear lad, you are quite cold and wet! Shivering, too, and incipient bronchitis in your voice. Come right away to the fire, and you shall have one of the doctor's coats and a glass of something hot.'

'Thanks; I must go and tell my aunt what has happened. She was not to sit up, but if she is awake she will be anxious.'

'You'll do no such thing! The woman would imagine Alison was drowned. Come away to the parlour, and I'll send Liz to tell Marget you are both here. You'll take your death if you go out in that condition. Does anyone know that it's Alison that's been making a fool of herself—doing an unwomanly thing?'

'No; they think it's a mill-girl,' the

x 2

poet answered, as he followed the lady into
the parlour.

'That's well; I'll caution Liz not to say
anything about it.'

In spite of the lateness of the hour, Liz
was delighted at the idea of an errand
that should give her the opportunity of
hearing more about the rescue. Not even
the high wind deterred her from going
out.

'I'll never keep my hat on,' she said
to herself; 'I'd better tie it on with a
hankie.'

But none of her handkerchiefs were
large enough for this, and she bethought
her of Dr. Murdoch's neckerchief that he
had used as a sling for Alison's arm. Liz
had a sentimental affection for the doctor,
and she had taken the neckerchief when
she removed from Well's Close as a sou-
venir of him. Now she took it out and

tied it over her hat, preparatory to braving the storm.

The Abbey House was not three minutes' walk from Mrs. Lindsay's, it would not take her long to go. But instead of going the nearest way, Liz turned into the High Street, where she met a group of girls taking Tibbie home.

In her drenched condition, with her hair streaming about her, Tibbie was not easily recognisable, but Liz's sharp eyes made her out at once.

'Fat's to dae wi' ye, Tibbie, siccan a sicht on yer merriage nicht?'

'Oh, Liz, dinna ye ken?' Bell Macniel sobbed. 'It's a sair nicht for her—her lad's awa'!'

'Jim?' said Liz, in an awe-struck tone. 'Is't him that's drooned i' the *Saucy Tib?*'

'Ay is't! an' I'm wae for the puir lassie.'

'Oh!' Liz cried wringing her hands

despairingly, 'what in a' the warld wull she dae the noo? Puir lassie! puir bonnie Tibbie!'

'I maun tak' her to her bed,' said Bell, moving on; 'she's wet through, puir lass!'

'Whaur's her shawlie?' Liz inquired.

'It's awa': she maun gae withoot it the noo——'

'Na, na; she shall hae a loan o' mine,' said Liz, taking off the neckerchief she had tied over her hat and putting it on Tibbie. 'Ta, ta, the noo; I maun rin to the Abbey Hoose, but I'll speer for you the morn, Tibbie, my lass.'

Liz hurried on, the tears rolling down her cheeks in sympathy for Tibbie, and feeling uncomfortable that she should have lent Dr. Murdoch's neckerchief, and so run the chance of Alison's discovering the theft.

Meanwhile, at Mrs. Lindsay's May was working havoc in two masculine hearts by her tender pride in Alison, and her tender solicitude for the two—Dr. Murdoch and the poet—who had been braving the elements. The doctor had returned to the house, and now May was proving herself a worthy daughter of her practical mother.

She brought slippers for the two; she mixed them a delicious concoction that looked like punch, but had a flavour about it of something diviner than toddy; she praised Alison and shed a few quiet tears for the girl whose lover was lost—in short, May was so unaffectedly womanly on this occasion that she appeared in a new light to the two men, who began to regard her as a ministering angel,

'A creature not too bright or good,
    For (preparing) human nature's daily food!'

From a matrimonial point of view it was

a thousand pities that May had become associated with Alison, for she had enough beauty and winsomeness to have attracted the other sex had she not been eclipsed by Alison's nobler charm. To these two, at least, she was perfect when Alison was not present to raise their ideals of perfection.

'The sort of woman,' the doctor said, as he stirred his punch, 'to make a man comfortable!'

'Less radiant, but less thorny than the rose,' said the poet, wistfully, remembering that Alison had never shown him any tender attention.

The doctor was tremendously elated. It was not ten hours since he had returned from his walk with Alison a disappointed man, thinking that the sun of his life had set; and here he was warming his feet at the fire and seeing the dawn of a new day in May Lindsay's glass of punch!

Mrs. Lindsay must have been right when she said that homœopathy was an effectual system in love-sickness only! He felt so philanthropical and humane that he told himself he was a fool; but his high spirits would not be frowned down, and he scandalised Mrs. Lindsay by displaying no solemnity at his escape from drowning. Once only he was grave. A chance allusion of May's to Jim sobered him instantly.

'It's the saddest thing I ever heard,' he said, 'and I'm awfully sorry for Mearns's lass. I almost wish that it had been any of the others rather than Jim.'

'Oh, Dr. Murdoch! The others are married; think of the women and children!' May exclaimed, reproachfully.

'Well, they might have got on better than Tibbie will. By the way, Mrs. Lindsay, did I tell you about old Swankie,

whose wife died last week? An auld
vixen that nearly raged the life out of
him?'

'No,' Mrs. Lindsay said, wondering at
the doctor's manner, and his evident desire
to avoid the subject of Tibbie.

'I'll tell you now, then. I met Mr.
Morrison to-night; he's their minister, and
he had been visiting the old fellow. Of
course he went prepared to administer re-
ligious consolation and all the rest of it,
but he found it wasn't wanted. When he
got to the house Swankie sat very lonely
in the chimney corner, the picture of
desolate bereavement; but when he saw
Morrison he turned round, rubbing his
hands and winking—"Eh, mon!" he says,
"it's a gey guid change syne you wis here
last!" Morrison didn't know what to say
to him, he was so dropped on; however,
he sat down, and after cracking a bit he

said he'd have a prayer with the old boy.
So they knelt down, and he prayed that
comfort might be administered to the
bereaved; the usual thing, you know.
Well, when they got up, Swankie seized
him by the shoulder and stared in his face
with a look of eager memory—"Dae ye
ken hoo muckle I lost waitin' on her?"
says he. "Twa stane!" Morrison can see
through a paving stone as far as anybody,
and he came away dying with laughing.
Old Swankie was right enough after all,
for she was what Liz would call "an orra-
lookin' trallap !" '

'I'll not have you talk like that of any
woman,' said Mrs. Lindsay, severely; 'wives
are only what their husbands make them.
You don't deserve that I should tell you
about Alison, and what she said.'

'What was it? Did she send me a
message?' he asked, eagerly.

'Yes. She said if it had not been for the whisky, she wouldn't have cried, and made herself too ill to go home to-night.'

Murdoch looked disappointed, and the poet rose to go.

'What am I to tell my aunt about this affair ?'

'Nothing !' Mrs. Lindsay said, definitely. 'Give her my love, and say I kept Alison to sleep with May. That's true enough : you needna look sceptical, Dr. Murdoch ! and that she'll be home to-morrow.'

May had noticed the poet's weary manner, and she felt sorry for him when he said dejectedly :

'Then I've done no good by waiting for Miss Alison !'

'Oh, yes, you have !' she cried, brightly.

"They also serve who only stand and wait."

Good-night, Mr. Robinson ; but stay ! you

shall have some lily-lamps to light you home.'

She took a bunch of lent-lilies from the table and gave them to the poet, whose feelings were too deep for words. May little knew that her quotation and her pretty fancy about the lilies were the tiny hinges on which hung the door of her fate. The poet's heart had hitherto held only a dainty volume bound in white and gold, and a vague hope of winning a dark-haired bride; but now there flitted into that dark chamber a fair presence, bearing a lily in her hand, for his heart's

> ' Gates of brass could not withstand
> One touch of that magic wand.'

Dante Algernon went out into the storm cherishing his lilies, and a hope fair as they that had blossomed that night for him.

And May tripped back into the parlour,

and lavished so much gentle sympathy
on the doctor that his heart—sore at
Alison's rejection, and jealous of Andrew
Rayne—was caught in the rebound. And
when Mrs. Lindsay left them a moment
together, and May looked at him with her
blue eyes full of tears, and with breaking
voice said how thankful she was he had
been spared, and what would she have
done if—— Well, then, neither quite
knew how it happened—perhaps the punch
had something to do with it!—then the
doctor drew her to him closely and pressed
his lips to hers, and said she was his sweet
little May, and would she be his dear little
wife? And May said 'Yes,' with a real
tremor in her voice, and a sudden terror
lest she was doing wrong and dooming
herself to a loveless marriage. Dr. Lindsay was from home, and nothing was said
to Mrs. Lindsay that night; but when one

o'clock rang out from the old church Murdoch went out into the storm carrying no lilies of hope, but a reckless despair in his heart, because he was pledged to marry the woman he did not love! And Alison slept with a smile on her lips, not knowing that May had won from her the love of two men who a few hours before had been willing to lay down their lives for her sake.

She smiled as she slept, for in the fishermen's homes that night happy women were praying God to bless the brave girl who had won their husbands from a watery grave.

She had won fame—and had lost the woman's crown of wedded love.

END OF THE FIRST VOLUME.

LONDON: PRINTED BY DUNCAN MACDONALD, BLENHEIM HOUSE.

BRITISH
22SE90
MUSEUM

Lightning Source UK Ltd.
Milton Keynes UK
UKHW030839020622
403888UK00007B/840